The Romantic Attack on Modern Science
in England and America
& Other Essays

Roger Sworder

The Romantic Attack
on Modern Science

in England and America
&
Other Essays

ANGELICO PRESS
SOPHIA PERENNIS

First published in the USA
by Angelico Press / Sophia Perennis
© Roger Sworder 2015

Series editor: James R. Wetmore

Angelico Press
4709 Briar Knoll Dr.
Kettering, OH 45429
www.angelicopress.com

ISBN 978-1-62138-147-1 (pbk)
ISBN 978-1-62138-148-8 (eBook)

Cover Image:
Adalbert Stifter, "Moonrise" (unfinished), ca. 1855
Cover Design: Michael Schrauzer

CONTENTS

Preface

For a long time now there has been a massive consensus among the universities of the West. They uniformly teach the theory of science—the empirical theory that appeared in England and France during the seventeenth and eighteenth centuries. This theory, and the many sciences it has encouraged, now command the Academy, and there are very few scholars who do not subscribe. The vast majority believes that the empirical sciences have given us a knowledge of the natural and human worlds unprecedented in human history. They believe these sciences now free us from many evils that burdened all previous generations. They suppose the new scientific method so reasonable and self-evident that it will win over all reasonable people, from whatever background, after due consideration. And they think this largely explains the inexorable spread of the new scientific order around the globe.

This massive consensus would be even more overwhelming were it not quite so deaf. Typically these new thinkers have chosen not to face their opponents but to ignore them. One egregious instance is John Locke's failure to mention Plato's theory of recollection in his protracted rebuttal of innate ideas. Locke had been a lecturer in Greek, but his omission here would fail the shortest undergraduate essay on the topic. More recently, many English and American poets have roundly denounced the new sciences, but though the works of these poets are taught in universities, this theme is not. Between the English and Philosophy departments, it has somehow dropped out of sight. The first essay in this book repairs this lapse by examining objections from six very famous poets to the new scientific theory.

And since we cannot be careful enough when we claim we know more than our ancestors did, the second piece opens with a quotation from Aristotle propounding accidental natural evolution; that is, living creatures are generated at random, and by pure chance some of them are fitted to survive and reproduce—and this is how we come to have the life-forms on earth. Aristotle did not accept this theory, but it was not beyond the wit of people twenty-three centuries ago to conceive of it. Similarly, we suppose now that our technological revolutions have sprung from our ingenuity, and that we were the first to think of these devices. But in ancient China and Rome, the labor-saving possibilities of automation were under discussion, together with the necessity for human labor. Their thoughts on these issues bear directly on the latest crisis of the new scientific order: systemic mass worklessness. And so the Miscellany concluding this volume deals with this and related themes.

Introduction

BLAKE, WORDSWORTH, AND COLERIDGE were epistemologists and philosophers of science. They were exponents of the intellect in the Classical and Medieval understanding of that term. When we think of the Romantics, we think of Nature and the passions. But Blake, Wordsworth, and Coleridge were arguably the last great English intellectuals.

'Intellect' is the English form of the Latin *intellectus,* which was the word used by the Latin Fathers of the Church to translate the Greek word *nous.* From 500 BC onwards, *nous* and then *intellectus* named the mental faculty which perceived Being. Being is without beginning or end, without past or future, unitary, continuous, all inclusive, and totally simultaneous. This is the being which *nous* or *intellectus* apprehends. And this was the theory of the intellect which these Romantics fought to defend as it was being displaced by the new Enlightenment conception of science. The English religious seemed largely powerless to resist this transformation in the understanding of science. These Romantics supplied the lack. They maintained the vision of science which began with Parmenides, Plato, and Aristotle, ran through Plotinus and the Greek and Latin Fathers, and on through the Middle Ages and the Renaissance.

The Romantics met the Enlightenment and faced it down. And they fought this struggle almost entirely at the level of principle, as epistemology, without regard to the material effects of the new sciences, good or bad. The Romantics stood at the doorway of the new science, with an adequate view both of what was passing and of what was to come in these changing theories of knowledge. They rejected the Enlightenment in favor of the much more thoroughly tested tradition from Parmenides onwards. In their writing they displayed again the Divine Being which intellect apprehends, in the context of the new science and in response to it. This is the Romantic intellect. On this view, the Romantic understanding was not rev-

3

olutionary nor preoccupied with the strange and exotic. It was strictly normative, a return to a long-established order.

In Germany, the Romantic intellectual was more common and more potent. Long before, Leibniz had written to Locke to question his empiricism, and had presented a theory of the mind which realized almost all the powers and properties of Being. Kant rejected David Hume's empiricist theory of perception. Novalis, born in the same year as Coleridge, wrote in his twenties a brief history of the struggle between the intellectual and material theories of science. Coleridge recited Wordsworth's *Intimations Ode* to Karl von Humboldt in Germany, and subscribed to a hierarchy of the sciences in which the ancient theory of intellection was the apex. This theory was far more developed in Germany than in England.

The epistemological genius of the English high Romantics did not grace England for long. John Keats' *Ode to Psyche* is one of its last and greatest achievements. But then this same Counter-Enlightenment broke out in America. In that gas-lit barbarism, according to Baudelaire, where progress was a kind of ecstasy for mugs, Edgar Allan Poe devoted himself to the self-same and eternal. The Transcendentalists transferred the full force of Plato and Plotinus onto the American soul. Well into the 20th century, Edwin Arlington Robinson attacked the nullity of the new science in terms as savage and as sharp as anyone since Blake. Robinson understood most bitterly how this new science denied any meaning or goal to human life.

ENGLAND

1

William Blake

I see the Past, Present & Future existing all at once
Before me. O Divine Spirit, sustain me on thy wings,
That I may awake Albion from his long & cold repose;
For Bacon & Newton, sheath'd in dismal steel, their terrors hang
Like iron scourges over Albion: Reasonings like vast Serpents
Infold around my limbs, bruising my minute articulations.

I turn my eyes to the Schools & Universities of Europe
And there behold the Loom of Locke, whose Woof rages dire,
Wash'd by the Water-wheels of Newton: black the cloth
In heavy wreathes folds over every Nation: cruel Works
Of many Wheels I view, wheel without wheel, with cogs tyrannic
Moving by compulsion each other, not as those in Eden, which,
Wheel within Wheel, in freedom revolve in harmony & peace.[1]

Did Blake see the future here? He watches as the academics of Europe generate a black cloth from the theories of Newton and Locke. He watches as this cloth covers every nation. As an idea, the new science has reached every corner of the globe, though not every nation has entirely succumbed. Could Blake reasonably have foreseen this in 1800? Just before the lines above, he writes of England as Albion:

> ... till the Twelve Sons of Albion
> Enrooted into every Nation, a Mighty Polypus growing
> From Albion over the whole Earth: such is my awful Vision.[2]

1. All quotations of Blake are taken from *Blake Complete Writings*, Geoffrey Keynes, 1972, Oxford, OUP, and are shown with the letter 'K' followed by the page number, initial of poem, plate number and/or line number. Thus: *K*. 635, *J*. 15:6.

2. *K*. 635, *J*. 15:3.

and later:

> Then all the Males conjoined into One Male, & every one
> Became a ravening eating Cancer growing in the Female,
> A Polypus of Roots, of Reasoning, Doubt, Despair & Death,
> Going forth & returning from Albion's Rocks to Canaan,
> Devouring Jerusalem from every Nation of the Earth.[3]

This is how Blake sees the English Enlightenment and the scientific revolution, as a huge amorphous growth that will cover and devour all spiritual aspiration in humankind; and it first appeared in England, which has therefore a world-historical role. This vision is lofty enough. And Blake turns his prophetic eye on the schools and universities of Europe. But he himself had almost no secondary and no tertiary education at all. Yet his tone here is far more authoritative than any vice-chancellor's. In that magisterial turning of his eyes to Europe's academies, we gain some idea of his elevation and intellectual power in the act of vision. He can turn his eyes anywhere and see with the same sense of eternity.

Blake does not anticipate the economic domination of the world by England here, but its spiritual disempowerment by English atheism. Why should he think this? Locke was a clergyman, and Bacon and Newton believing Christians. Why should Blake suppose that their science would be so demoralizing? The reason is in the image of the loom mechanically driven by water-wheels, and this reason is repeated in the account of the cogs and wheels under compulsion at the end. There is an industrial dimension here. Could Blake have foreseen how industrializing mercers of Manchester would overshadow India's domestic textiles? Perhaps he did if we take that black cloth literally. But the cloth is primarily a symbol of the intellectual benightedness which Blake believes the new science to bring. The new science is satisfied with mechanical explanations only. Water-wheels generally powered grinding mills for grains and this arrangement was also used by Novalis to represent the new science:

> With some difficulty it placed man first in the order of created things, and reduced the infinite creative music of the universe to

---

3. *K. 707, J.* 69:1.

the monotonous clatter of a monstrous mill, which, driven by the stream of chance and floating thereon, was supposed to be a mill in the abstract, without Builder or Miller, in fact an actual *perpetuum mobile,* a mill that milled of itself.[4]

For Blake, the horror of the idea lay in the compulsion. The Platonic view, for example, maintained that the stars are divine intelligences whose regularity of motion is due to their much greater spiritual development. What the Newtonians had done was to turn everything into a play of mechanical forces only.

Blake's vision of the British Empire-to-be stands in sharp contrast, say, to the grand vision of the Roman Empire sung by Vergil. Britain's pre-eminence is a matter for horror in Blake's view. But Albion too is under terrible punishment: 'For Bacon & Newton, sheath'd in dismal steel, their terrors hang Like iron scourges over Albion.' This too is a symbol of mental submission to the theories of Bacon and Newton. But as with the black cloth, it resonates now with what was to happen to Blake's Albion in history. London was the first city to suffer a prolonged and intensive bombing blitz from aeroplanes. Are those aeroplanes the iron scourges of Bacon & Newton? Bacon had envisaged flying machines, and Newton's parallelogram of the forces of gravity and inertia is a principle of ballistics. When aeroplanes drop their bombs, they devastate a strip of land as the bombs fall successively in the same direction. The marks of a whip or scourge on a human body are similar. Now the giant Albion is physically present to us. And England, of course, has been under constant aerial threat for much of the time since.

Blake's prophecies are certainly suggestive, but are they intellectual as I have defined it? Are they perceptions of that Being without beginning or end, without past or future? At the very least we must say that his prophecies universalize the struggles in his time between belief and unbelief, which is as much a feature of Platonic as of Christian writers. Blake's historical thesis concerning Albion is as vast as it is heterodox. But all that we actually see of Heaven here

4. Novalis, *Hymns to the Night and Other Selected Writings,* "Christendom Or Europe", tr. C.E. Passant, 1960, USA: The Liberal Arts Press, p. 45.

is the last lines of the opening quotation, where, wheel within wheel, the Edenic cogs revolve in freedom, harmony and peace.

Violent though Blake's account of the future is, with its iron scourges and driven cogs, the poet himself is dispassionate in its midst. He sees these terrible things and describes them like a pharaoh from his throne. There is nothing trancelike. It is sharp and immediate, but the mind which perceives at once denounces and transcends. In this next passage, the prophet appears before us incandescent, in the fullest possible self-affirmation of himself as divine and divinely inspired. He is a resurrected Milton, aware of scientific and artistic developments in the century and more since his death, and now returned to repudiate them. He is appalled at how the divine art of poetry as prophecy has been traduced. This Milton is the Blake of those last verses in the short hymn *Jerusalem*, with his sword and bow and chariot of fire. This is the mental fight at full stretch. He starts like a Homeric hero, like Achilles or Odysseus among his enemies:

> ... in terrible majesty Milton
> Replied: Obey thou the Words of the Inspired Man.
> All that can be annihilated must be annihilated
> That the Children of Jerusalem may be saved from slavery.
> There is a Negation, & there is a Contrary:
> The negation must be destroy'd to redeem the Contraries.
> The negation is the Spectre, the Reasoning Power in Man:
> This is a false Body, an Incrustation over my Immortal
> Spirit, a Selfhood which must be put off & annihilated alway.
> To cleanse the Face of my Spirit by Self-examination,
> To bathe in the Waters of Life, to wash off the Not Human,
> I come in Self-annihilation & the grandeur of Inspiration,
> To cast off Rational Demonstration by Faith in the Saviour,
> To cast off the rotten rags of Memory by Inspiration,
> To cast off Bacon, Locke & Newton from Albion's covering,
> To take off his filthy garments & clothe him with Imagination,
> To cast aside from Poetry all that is not Inspiration,
> That it no longer shall dare to mock with the aspersion of Madness
> Cast on the Inspired by the tame high finisher of paltry Blots
> Indefinite, or paltry Rhymes, or paltry Harmonies,
> Who creeps into State Government like a catterpiller to destroy;

To cast off the idiot Questioner who is always questioning
But never capable of answering, who sits with a sly grin
Silent plotting when to question, like a thief in a cave,
Who publishes doubt & calls it knowledge, whose Science is
    Despair,
Whose pretence to knowledge is envy, whose whole Science is
To destroy the wisdom of ages to gratify ravenous Envy
That rages round him like a Wolf day & night without rest:
He smiles with condescension, he talks of Benevolence & Virtue,
And those who act with Benevolence & Virtue they murder time
    on time.
These are the destroyers of Jerusalem, these are the murderers
Of Jesus, who deny the Faith & mock at Eternal life,
Who pretend to Poetry that they may destroy Imagination
By imitation of Nature's Images drawn from Remembrance.
These are the Sexual Garments, the Abomination of Desolation,
Hiding the Human Lineaments as with an Ark & Curtains
Which Jesus rent & now shall wholly purge away with Fire
Till Generation is swallow'd up in Regeneration.[5]

To read these lines aloud is not easy. Emotionally the passage is *fortissimo,* from the seventh or eighth line, and remains so to the end. It seems to require a more than mortal energy to deliver so prolonged a climax. And it is very destructive, with the terrible fires of regeneration at the end. Blake in the person of the resurrected Milton tears down the science, philosophy, painting, poetry, music, morality and social justice of England at the turn of the 19th century. And at the end Jesus sets what is left of it on fire. Blake is in the full fury of prophetic inspiration and the passage displays the prophet in his self-disclosure as the way to delivering its message. Jesus, Jerusalem and the prophetic mode suggest Judaism and Christianity, but this presentation of the prophet has perhaps most in common with Empedocles' account of himself at the beginning of the *Purifications.* Blake's verses are Old Testament prophecy recast as Epic hexameters in the Greek and Roman grand archaic style.

    With the two words 'I come', Blake declares as his mission the

---

5. *K.* 532–533, *M.* 2:40–41.

destruction of English culture. To do this is why he exists. He reaffirms it in the passage from *Jerusalem* where he has come to awaken Albion from his long and cold repose. As the manner of the Sicilian Empedocles was most like Blake's in this passage, so Blake's mission has much in common with that of Athenian Socrates and his account of himself in his *Apology*. Socrates, too, had a mission to his people which was typically destructive. He called himself a gadfly whom God had sent to stir the lazy Athenians into some mental activity.

To vow oneself to the utter destruction of the age in which one lives takes a certain self-assurance. Is it arrogance? We remember that Blake is speaking as Milton here, a Milton who has returned from more than a hundred years in the beyond. This gives some immediate color to Blake's claims of self-annihilation and of his being only immortal spirit. But he is more than mediumistic or even prophetic, he is messianic. The passage as a whole turns on his metaphor of casting out, and this recalls Jesus's casting of the money-changers out of the temple. And at the end Jesus, at whose death the curtain in the temple was torn in two, joins with, or is, this Miltonic Blake as he destroys that curtain with fire. This moment is a Blakean eternity. Compare how we read of Armageddon and the Second Coming in St. Matthew, but then see it happen in the first martyrdom in the Acts. As Stephen is stoned to death, he sees the return of the Son on the right hand of the Father. In the same way, the destruction of the temple curtain and the revelation of the inner mystery is Jesus's work in eternity, now and forever and not only at the very end of all.

Blake is possessed by Milton, the only English epic poet, and is merely the resurrected Milton's agent. This is a self-effacement. But there is a greater self-naughting than this in the passage. The poet's destruction of the mental world of his time is matched by the continuous destruction of his own selfhood which is what the reasoning spectre for ever weaves around him. This is the inner Jihad against oneself as contrasted with the outer Jihad against the world. But both these Jihads are mental fights. Blake or Milton speaks here as an immortal spirit, and from that point of view ones own selfhood is even more to be destroyed than spiritual error in the world at large. It is even more 'to be put off and annihilated alway.' This is the meaning of the cleansing and bathing processes. The 'not Human' is the spiritual defilement of the selfish reasoner, to which the speaker is himself continually tempted and from which he arises here triumphant and truly a man.

Still, the downright rejection of reason and rational demonstration is hard for us to take. But it is a standard thesis from Socrates onwards that intellection is the higher function since intellection perceives the absolute. So geometers draw figures and demonstrate theorems, but philosophers take these terms of the mathematical sciences as springboards to gain a vision of their place in eternity. Those who make no such efforts at all are like prisoners bound to posts in a cave and their lives are spent in futile competition as they guess the order of shadows projected in front of them. Is this in part the origin of Blake's metaphor of incrustation, the Platonic prisoners in their cave? For Aristotle the highest human activity, the one to which the rest of a human life ideally conduces is 'the thinking of thinking', a reabsorption into the greatest powers of the mind. In the Christian order this inwardness is the Kingdom of Heaven and to attain it is to experience the beatific vision.

Which is prior, reason or intellection? Which should judge the other? Traditionally there is no question but that intellection, *noesis*, is ultimate and primordial. The aspiration to such knowledge is the principle of learning and human development. And so the tag *Credo ut intelligam*, 'I believe so that I may understand.' The reason does not sit in judgement on this faith. Blake's mythic story in his long poems is largely the story of how Reason ran amok, wreaked havoc and was finally brought back to its place among the faculties.

Inspiration and faith in the Saviour are here identified with imagination. These are the preconditions of true science. Blake objected to the Classical parentage of the Muses, saying that Memory could only produce naturalistic images. But he had some confidence in Plato's account of divine inspiration in the *Ion* and the *Phaedrus*:

The Ancients did not mean to Impose when they affirm'd their belief in Vision & Revelation. Plato was in Earnest: Milton was in Earnest. They believ'd That God did Visit Man Really & Truly. . . .[6]

Where the Greeks and Romans talked of the Muses and inspiration, the Christians talked of the Holy Spirit and grace. At crucial and difficult moments Blake will invoke the aid of the Divine Spirit. Blake attacks the Enlightenment for attempting to usurp the prerogatives of intellection. Reason has broken the framework of the faculties and is now dominant. Reason glories in its freedom from those obsolete constraints and in its presumption of powers and honours long denied it. This is the figure which Blake must fight.

But in that case reason has a place, it is not just negation. And at the conclusion of the long poem *Jerusalem* reason again takes its seat as president of the arts and sciences. But in the meanwhile it has usurped the positions of Urthona and Los, the divine creative imagination which apprehends the eternal ideas. It is this extension of reason's power over the territory of its betters which is absolute nullity. When reason claims to know that there is nothing but matter, and denies the scriptures, it errs. It has usurped the role of another faculty and so far it is a nothing. Blake compounds two different notions here. First, there is that seemingly endless ratiocination about one's own interests which occupies our minds willy-nilly. This is the spectre, the reasoning power, which must be constantly destroyed. Then there is the new Enlightenment science which strips the world of intellection and imagination, and leaves it no more than a play of indifferent forces. Blake sees these as identical under the description of the reasoning power in man. The new science is the old Adam.

From this angle, Blake's claim that the purpose of the new science is to destroy the wisdom of ages to gratify ravenous envy makes good sense. Blake's rejection of the new science is difficult for us to follow when he calls it negation and attributes it to envy. How can it be negation when we see the plethora of its achievements? It has transformed the world. Yes, but it has not added an iota to the real-

6. *K.* 473.

ization of our spiritual destiny except to confuse and befuddle. And worse, it tries to smash the forms of understanding by which visionary humans can live. For Blake faith in the Saviour is far more essential to science than rational demonstration, but for Enlightenment thinkers this is the superstition of Scholastics. Many scientists suppose that one unalloyed benefit of the new science is that it freed us from superstition.

When we turn with Blake from the filthy garments of the sciences to the arts, we encounter a poetry, too, which mocks inspiration and calls it madness. This was a word used often about Blake himself and his whole-hearted belief in heavenly guidance. I quoted Blake's approval of Plato's belief in inspiration, and it is relevant to Blake's defence against these aspersions on his sanity. For Plato believed that divine madness was responsible for any number of enormous benefits to humankind, and that we could hardly survive without it. This must have warmed Blake's heart. As for the poets who mocked inspiration, they sound like the sterile Augustan Classicists of the 18th century whose invocations of the ancient godlings Blake had come to reject decisively a year or so before he began *Milton*. Of these poets who followed French models, Keats was to write that they swayed about upon a rocking-horse and called it Pegasus.

For Blake the major exponent of reason in the arts, as opposed to the sciences, was Sir Joshua Reynolds, a leading painter of that time. Sir Joshua had been honoured by the King with the task of founding a Royal Academy of the arts and he had published the discourses he delivered to that academy. Blake wrote extensive comments on his copy of these discourses, in which he criticized Reynolds' theories on the same grounds that he attacked the new scientists:

> Burke's Treatise on the Sublime & Beautiful is founded on the Opinions of Newton & Locke; on this Treatise Reynolds has grounded many of his assertions in all his Discourses. I read Burke's Treatise when very Young; at the same time I read Locke on Human Understanding & Bacon's Advancement of Learning; on Every one of these Books I wrote my Opinions, & looking them over find that my Notes on Reynolds in this Book are exactly Similar. I felt the Same Contempt & Abhorrence then that I do now. They mock Inspiration & Vision. Inspiration & Vision was then, &

now is, & I hope will always Remain, My Element, my Eternal
Dwelling place; how can I then hear it Contemned without returning Scorn for Scorn?[7]

For Blake, this is very temperate. It mentions but does not display
his scorn. But in the climax from *Milton*, the Miltonic Blake casti-
gates the poetry, painting and music of his time by twice repeating
'paltry.' It is all tame, high finish and blots and vagueness. Blake was
fond of calling Rubens' work 'the Flemish ooze.' It is a pity he may
never have heard Reynolds called 'Sir Sloshua'!

We come now to a very difficult line in the climax of *Milton*:

Who creeps into State government like a catterpiller to destroy.

The line is difficult in two ways. First it comes at the end of eleven
lines which are a single sentence. The breath control required is
considerable. And then the mention of the caterpillar is in danger of
bathos. This is unfortunate because it risks damage to a speech
which realizes intellectual *furor* to an unusual degree. An explanation for the line is not far to seek. At the beginning of his copy of
Reynolds' *Discourses* Blake wrote:

Having spent the Vigour of my Youth & Genius under the oppres-
sion of Sr Joshua & his Gang of Cunning Hired Knaves Without
Employment & as much as could possibly be Without Bread, The
Reader must Expect to Read in all my Remarks on these Books
Nothing but Indignation & Resentment. While Sr Joshua was rolling in Riches, Barry was Poor & unemploy'd except by his own
Energy; Mortimer was call'd a Madman, & only Portrait Painting
applauded & rewarded by the Rich & Great. Reynolds & Gainsbor-
ough Blotted & Blurred one against the other & Divided all the
English World between them. Fuseli, Indignant, almost hid him-
self. I am hid.[8]

So Blake saw the Royal Academy. Beyond the objections here was
another: the Royal Academy did not admit engravers into full
membership. Blake was excluded as a professional by the rules. That

7. *K.* 476–477.
8. *K.* 445.

16

aside, depriving capable artisans of their livelihood is a very serious injustice and Blake cites his evidence. The new Academy brought about a disturbance in the normative values of Blake's workplace which threatened him directly. So much for State government and Reynolds, its parasite. The four syllables of 'catterpiller' illustrate his creeping motion.

We may divide Milton's long speech here into two halves. The first half ends with the catterpiller in State government; the second half begins with the idiot questioner. In the first half Blake begins by attacking the reasoning power, rational demonstration, and Bacon, Newton and Locke. He then transfers his attack from the sciences to the arts without a pause. This transition is bridged by the rejection of inspiration by the arts as well as the sciences. And we can see how for Blake the Reynolds of the *Discourses* seamlessly connects the corruption of the sciences to the corruption of the arts. For his *Discourses* drew upon Burke, in Blake's opinion, and Burke depended on Newton and Locke. In the second half of Milton's speech, Blake returns to his attack on the sciences as the idiot questioner becomes the publisher of doubt and the scientist of despair. But then Blake moves in a new direction and attacks the condescending smiler who talks of benevolence and virtue, and we are told that such people murder Jesus time on time and destroy Jerusalem.

Let A stand for an attack on science; B for an attack on the arts; C for an attack on smiling condescension, benevolence and virtue. Then the first half of Milton's speech is AB and the second half is ACB. For Milton returns to the arts at the end of his speech. We have seen how the transition from A to B has its own clear logic in the shared rejection of inspiration by the arts as well as the sciences. But we have also seen how the figure of Reynolds is one exemplar to Blake of how the arts and sciences are suffering from the same defect. Similarly with the transition in the second half from Milton's second attack on the sciences to his attack on smiling condescension, benevolence and virtue. The logical connection is clear enough: the science is Godless and the benevolence soulless. Neither the science nor the benevolence recognizes the divine core. Not to recognize the divinity in others is to murder them in the spirit whatever you do to their bodies. But again, as with Reynolds, there is an exemplar here of the link between the new science and the new secular ethics.

Voltaire, it was said, always smiled but never laughed. He is the smiler here. Voltaire had spent some time in England and had composed his *Philosophical Letters* as a commentary on the English. He wrote there at length on Newton and Locke and praised them. He admired the tolerance shown religious nonconformity in England. But with the character of Dr. Pangloss in *Candide*, he lampooned the belief that everything is for the best in the best of all possible worlds. Instead, he demonstrated the violence and brutality both in nature and in humanity. Blake presented Voltaire as a mocker, a man incapable of seeing the divinity around him and engaged in its vain denial. For Blake the art of human relations consisted precisely in recognizing the divinity of others. So 'cherish pity lest you turn an angel from your door.' And we remember St Paul's words about good works which lack charity and love as 'sounding brass and clashing cymbal.'

I have taken several pages to discuss Milton's speech which takes a page or so. The speech covers many topics and the mere act of attending to it for so long will of itself have brought it into focus. I mentioned before the imperious tone of 'I turn my eyes to the schools and universities of Europe.' This speech has the same authority, an authority easy for us to accept, given the range and clarity of his denunciation. That strictly it is the resurrected Milton who speaks helps to temper our sense of Blake's arrogance. That the position adopted by the speaker requires the constant annihilation of the speaker's own selfhood tempers that sense still further. But the breadth and range of the issues considered, the depth at which they are understood and the coherence between them all combine to induce an alteration of the vision and a clarification. One man still stands there finally, amid the wreckage of his culture:

> Ye are the salt of the earth: but if the salt hath lost his savour, wherewith shall it be salted? It is thenceforth good for nothing, but to be cast out and to be trodden under foot of men.[9]

9. Matthew 5:13.

🌴

From one point of view, these passages from Blake's *Jerusalem* and *Milton* are the rant of a Christian fundamentalist. Milton's speech is a rant since no normal human voice can sustain it throughout its length at the pitch and with the intensity needed. It is fundamentalist because it prefers scriptural revelation to rational science, and it is Christian because it draws its symbols and metaphors from the Judaeo-Christian tradition. But Blake was a fundamentalist's fundamentalist. He was so extreme in his own convictions that nobody at all could share his religion with him. One of those convictions was the ironic reading of scripture by which God and Satan, angels and devils, heaven and hell, virtue and vice each changed places with the other at the most alarming speed. Another was his peculiar form of Unitarianism. Unitarians do not believe that Jesus was or is divine; only God is. But Blake did not believe that God was or is divine; only Jesus is.

Again, it may be said of all these passages from *Jerusalem* and *Milton* that they are unrelievedly negative, though this, of course, may be due to my selection rather than Blake's general tone. But even granted the selection is not typical, the negativity of Milton's speech at the climax of that poem suggests that Blake is not contemplating the divine being here, but grinding an axe, indeed a great many axes. I can just see Blake's monumental drawing of this figure, and very dark and malign he is! Did not Blake himself show again and again how everything that lives is holy? How then does he come so fiercely to denounce the sciences, the arts and the concern for others' welfare all around him? How can he trash so much when he claims it is all sacred?

These objections do not do full justice to the scope and intensity of Blake's negativity in these passages. Blake does not merely condemn certain corruptions, as he sees them, in his own place and time. He sees the new science as changing the whole world, not materially but spiritually. It will cover the globe like a black cloth and cancerously devour the human sense of the divine. This is a millennarian or eschatological vision of world-historical power, though it is no more than the wilder proponents of the Enlightenment had hoped for from Bacon onwards. Blake saw that they were right and was horrified. So he is filled with a much greater dread and with much better reason. Clearly he does not think he is likely to stop it. His vision is of its victory and yet he fights. We have now Hector near his end, rather than Achilles or Odysseus. Albion has already succumbed. Can Blake save the rest of the world?

It is one thing not to believe in the intellect and its vision. It is also possible to believe in it too readily. This is the error of supposing that the holiness of everything is easily grasped. In fact it is the pearl of great price for which we should give everything that we have. We have to seek it with all our strength and even that is not enough, without the supervention of divine madness or grace. What Blake saw in his time was the closing of many avenues to the intellect. Science no longer recognized that vision as its ultimate goal. The arts no longer believed that their inspiration opened heaven to them. Christian charity was yielding to an impersonal order which did not recognize the divine in others. Certainly a society is more or less open to heaven, and it may close itself away from the vision it once had. Against this closing Blake fought his mental fight believing his enemies were holy too, despite their denying it.

And there is surely a certain liberating charge in the devastation Blake's Milton creates around himself. This charge is felt by many readers of *The Marriage of Heaven and Hell* where Blake's whole-hearted adoption of the Devil's persona, the sheer outrage of it all, is like no other book on offer. But there, as we throw off every moral injunction and invert every sacred teaching, we are liberating sensual desire from the menacing priests. And this is attractive to many. With *Milton* we are far beyond that, as the very last lines of his speech show. The lines on the sexual garments as the abomination of desolation suggest that Blake is retreading the path of the metaphysical poets. These often deplored in later poems their libertine excesses in earlier ones. But a delighted shock of outrage is common to Milton's speech and the *Marriage*. The prophetic figure of Milton's speech appeals to fewer than the witty Satanism, but for those few the shock of delight is much greater than even the *Marriage* gives.

Those few are the intellectuals of each succeeding generation as they stand on a rock slowly disappearing beneath a sea of unbelief. For them, Blake's negativity is utterly bracing, a real friend in the loneliest of places. Reading these lines of Blake, they grasp the scope of his antipathy to the thinking and feeling of his time, because they have felt the same for what surrounds them for most of their lives. They take an actual pleasure in how clearly and comprehensively Blake tears down those pretensions to science, art and the care of others. It is not the pure pleasure which art sometimes offers, but a mixed pleasure which has been a grim suffering.

2

William Wordsworth

COLERIDGE READ OUT Wordsworth's *Ode Intimations of Immortality: Recollections of Early Childhood* to Karl Willem von Humboldt in Germany. Some twenty years later Crabbe Robinson read the poem to Blake who was deeply moved by it. I give here the ninth of its eleven parts:

> Oh joy! that in our embers
> Is something that doth live,
> That Nature yet remembers
> What was so fugitive!
> The thought of our past years in me doth breed
> Perpetual benediction: not indeed
> For that which is most worthy to be blest;
> Delight and liberty, the simple creed
> Of Childhood, whether busy or at rest,
> With new-fledged hope still fluttering in his breast:
> Not for these I raise
> The song of thanks and praise;
> But for those obstinate questionings
> Of sense and outward things,
> Fallings from us, vanishings;
> Blank misgivings of a Creature
> Moving about in worlds not realized,
> High instincts before which our mortal Nature
> Did tremble like a guilty Thing surprised:
> But for those first affections,
> Those shadowy recollections,
> Which, be they what they may,
> Are yet the fountain light of all our day,
> Are yet a master light of all our seeing;

> Uphold us, cherish, and have power to make
> Our noisy years seem moments in the being
> Of the eternal Silence: truths that wake,
>   To perish never;
> Which neither listlessness, nor mad endeavour,
>   Nor Man nor Boy,
> Nor all that is at enmity with joy.
> Can utterly abolish or destroy!
>   Hence in a season of calm weather
>   Though inland far we be,
> Our Souls have sight of that immortal sea
>   Which brought us hither,
>   Can in a moment travel thither,
> And see the Children sport upon the shore,
> And hear the mighty waters rolling evermore.[1]

Von Humboldt was surprised by the poem because, although its style was distinctive, he had not heard of the poet. He supposed it very much like the work of the Elizabethan poets, and this was astute. The lines above are as Platonic as any English verses since Henry Vaughan's *The World*. Elsewhere in the poem, Wordsworth's conception of infancy as heaven recalls Vaughan's *The Retreate:*

> Happy those early dayes! when I
> Shin'd in my Angell-infancy.

There is nothing in the eleven sections of Wordsworth's poem to date it to the turn of the 19th century, except the minor features of its diction and typography. So we will not find in this poem that characteristic of the Romantic intellectual, an explicit response to the challenge of the Enlightenment. For that response we must look elsewhere in Wordsworth's writing. He is speaking here of intellectual intuition as profoundly as any thinker in the tradition, and the new science is not at issue, though it is, perhaps, an underlying spur.

The first line invokes joy. In this Wordsworth is with Blake and Coleridge and the whole of the intellectual tradition. Parmenides described how his lesson in Being began with a chariot ride as far as

---

1. Wordsworth, W., *The Poetical Works of Wordsworth*, Ed: Thomas Hutchinson, 1934, London, OUP, pp. 461–462.

desire could reach. For Plato and Aristotle wisdom was the supreme human pleasure. In the Hindu tradition '*chit*' which is intellect and '*sat*' which is Being are bound to each other and to '*ananda*', joy. Joy is the accompaniment of intellection. But this power of Joy is only invoked here. We knew it as children and it is still just there in our burnt-out hearts. Wordsworth is concerned with the embers of childhood joy which we retain and not the childhood joy itself. These embers still in our hearts are enough to alienate us from our experiences as adults. Because we once saw as visionaries, we cannot adapt to the common light of day. We cannot finally accept our transience and mortality. This anxiety and sense of estrangement from the temporal order were for Wordsworth the most powerful reason for thankfulness. Existential angst was the one thing above all for which Wordsworth thanked Heaven. For it was the most certain evidence that in childhood he had seen more clearly. Why otherwise should he be so disconcerted by his adult lack of understanding?

How do people and things just vanish? Why does the world not make sense? Why do I feel demands of conscience? Wordsworth universalizes these questions and makes them ours, not his alone, throughout the passage. This kind of self-questioning he takes to be the common practice of humankind and there he may be a little optimistic. But it is likely to be the common practice of those who read his poems. Socrates, of course, was expert at exploiting the incoherence of sense perception as was Zeno of Elea. But they did not suppose, as Wordsworth did, that we were the best philosophers when we were six years old. Socrates and Plato supposed that the years of physical growth were dominated by unorganized energy, and it was not until maturity that the body settled enough to allow contemplative thoughts. At that time, the incoherence in our understandings could be demonstrated to us, and we could begin to make progress in philosophy.

That we do not feel at home here means that we must have felt at home somewhere else. The argument is not unlike one of Blake's. Since human desire is infinite, the infinite must be its fulfilment or our lot is despair. Blake too believed in the divinity of childhood and traces the closing of the innocent eye through the sufferings of experience. But there is in Wordsworth's line about blank misgivings a quite new expression of the human predicament as alien-ation. To see oneself as a creature moving about in worlds not realized is to be much more lost than Hamlet, who is trapped by cir-cumstance and not by the human condition. But far from repre-senting the human state *in toto*, Wordsworth's misgivings are merely the evidence that once he had none.

Can this be right? Are we really to suppose that these indetermi-nate misgivings we feel are themselves evidence of a higher state of being which we have largely misplaced? This is not how many exis-tentialists understood the problem. They took that initial bewilder-ment to be a more adequate response to our situation than a trust in some certainty which that bewilderment may or may not presup-pose. But since they give no real explanation of how that bewilder-ment arises, Wordsworth's dialectic may after all be the more subtle. The play between bewilderment and joy in these lines is the inverse corollary of Keats' claim that melancholy is at the center of delight. Here joy is at the center of the obstinate questions and blank mis-givings. Wordsworth's interpretation of his confusion is strikingly different from how Sartre and Camus saw theirs. They took their confusion to register precisely the absurdity around them, and there was no sense to be had of it at all.

The obstinate questionings and the blank misgivings are signs of something lost. The high instincts are a positive sign. For Kant the conscience was the best evidence of the Divine. And just as positive are the first affections and the shadowy recollections. Those who know Wordsworth will know that these affections and recollections spring from the formative visions of his childhood, recollected as an adult in tranquillity. They are those moments described with pas-sion in *Daffodils* and *The Prelude*. But as we have already learnt in the *Intimations Ode*, the child has these visions because it has so recently arrived from God and the imperial palace of our pre-exist-ence. As a Christian, Wordsworth was heterodox here, since it is not part of Christian belief that the soul pre-exists its life on earth. This opens the way to the possibility of reincarnation. While Word-sworth certainly claims pre-existence, that pre-existence is not another mortal life, nor yet those worlds between lives experienced by Plato's souls. We are then with God. So Wordsworth's heterodoxy is limited. But we must take it, I think, that the shadowy recollections are not merely memories of formative moments in childhood, but Platonic recollections of the great principles which we knew when with God. We are shown in what follows that these recollections are very powerful but they are not specified further. 'Be they what they may.' On the other hand, the repeated demonstrative 'those' seems to make them concrete and familiar.

From the obstinate questionings to the shadowy recollections we have a series of intimations. They are the fountain-light and master-light of all our seeing. Clearly these intimations are not a physical light or lights, yet they are the principle of all our seeing. This echoes Plato's theory of ideas. We see what we see here in the world by virtue of eternal ideas after which are formed whatever we experience through the senses. These eternal ideas are apprehended by intellect which understands how they are united in Being. Plato calls this last realization the vision of the Idea of the Good. In this principle are the ideas and after the ideas are modelled all the forms of creatures in the physical creation. So the Idea of the Good is the principle of all experience, not just seeing, though Plato propounds his theory by a series of visual analogies. This same theory is encapsulated in the motto of Oxford University, *Dominus Illuminatio Mea*, The Lord is my Light.

Wordsworth really does claim in this poem that we are at our best as philosophers when we are six years old. So the fact that our study of Plato at that age is usually nonexistent is no barrier at all to our apprehension of Being. This view has little sanction in the Graeco-Roman tradition but a very central place in Christianity, since Christ taught that we cannot enter Heaven unless we become like little children. So the first affections and shadowy recollections may, indeed, be the foundation of all our seeing and understanding. Coleridge, though he loved the poem, had reservations at just this point. Why, he complained, do I remember the trivial things from my childhood, while treasures of wisdom like this have disappeared without trace? From this point of view Wordsworth's consistent universalization of his understanding is tendentious.

These truths 'wake.' They are not learnt but are latent. Nor do they perish. And they have the power to lead us back to the source.

There follow here not one but two accounts of our relations with eternity. According to the first, these truths have the power to make our temporal experiences seem no more than moments in Being. They are not lost in eternity but reside there. The expression 'the Being of the eternal silence' takes everything away with the silence which could be an eternal vacuum or nullity, until we consider its being. Then we realize that in that state what we have been here enters into the entirely new dialectic of the absolute. And that order is perfect power. These are the hardest topics of all on which to write and Wordsworth is quite simple.

The second account of eternity turns upon an image drawn from seeing rather than hearing. Here our being far inland is a metaphor of our adult estrangement from the source. The sense of astral travel as we move, however far, from the inland to the coast in an instant, gives a marvellous sense of power. Our arrival at that shore was birth, and since then we have been moving upcountry as we age. But we may return to our source in moments of tranquillity and remember our innocent wisdom as children. It is striking that these two images of eternity, the auditory and the visual, are actually contradictory, since the eternal silence of the first is followed by the mighty rolling of the waters in the second. And this too is right because the images serve more adequately in their contradiction than if they agreed.

In the Preface to the *Lyrical Ballads,* published in the same year as the *Intimations Ode* was begun, Wordsworth discusses the relationship between poetry and the new science:

> The objects of the poet's thoughts are everywhere; though the eyes and senses of man are, it is true, his favourite guides, yet he will follow wheresoever he can find an atmosphere of sensation in which to move his wings. Poetry is the first and last of all knowledge—it as immortal as the heart of man. If the labours of men of science should ever create any material revolution, direct or indirect, in our condition, and in the impressions which we habitually receive, the poet will sleep then no more than at present, but he

will be ready to follow the steps of the man of science, not only in those general indirect effects, but he will be at his side, carrying sensation into the midst of the objects of the science itself. The remotest discoveries of the chemist, the botanist, or mineralogist, will be as proper objects of the poet's art as any upon which it can be employed, if the time should ever come when these things shall be familiar to us, and the relations under which they are contemplated by the followers of these respective sciences shall be manifestly and palpably material to us as enjoying and suffering beings. If the time should ever come when what is now called science, thus familiarized to men, shall be ready to put on, as it were, a form of flesh and blood, the poet will lend his divine spirit to aid the transfiguration, and will welcome the being thus produced, as a dear and genuine inmate of the household of Man.[2]

At first sight this is accommodating. Though poetry is the first and last of all knowledge, Wordsworth anticipates cooperation between the poet and the scientist. He does not set them at each others' throats as Blake does. But on closer examination Wordsworth's meaning is less straightforward. Three times he states the conditional 'if the time should ever come.' He writes 'if' here, not 'when.' He qualifies the possibility still further with 'ever', and he does it three times. Surely the implication of the grammar is that this time may never come. Certainly, we can be quite sure that it has not come yet.

Why not? Copernicus and Galileo, Harvey and Bacon, Newton and Boyle had all made important scientific discoveries or framed scientific theory. What was holding the poets back? The Royal Society had been established for nearly a century and a half when Wordsworth wrote these words. Why were there not more poems celebrating their insights and bringing them to life for humanity at large? And what did Wordsworth himself contribute in this regard? The answer is almost nothing, and it is true of almost all the poets since Wordsworth too. Yet surely there can be no doubt by now that the new sciences have created a material revolution, direct and indirect, in our condition and in the impressions we habitually receive.

2. Ibid, p. 738.

The cause of the impasse in Wordsworth's view is not hard to find, though it is implied and not stated. The poet will follow wherever he can find an atmosphere of sensation in which he can move his wings. He will one day perhaps be at the scientist's side carrying sensation into the midst of the objects of the science itself. But the objects of chemistry and mineralogy, as the new sciences understand them, the elements and the atoms, do not actually feel. And indeed the idea of subjective experience itself is problematical for the new sciences. The phenomenon of consciousness is and has been an impediment to the free march of empirical analysis. The capacity to feel is exactly what the new scientist does not want brought into the objects of his study. The ancients had understood the stars and planets to be divine intelligences, great gods of destiny, but this was just the kind of superstition that the new sciences of blind force would obviate. Likewise, Descartes and, we hope, the vivisectionists believed that animals were machines incapable of pain.

So Wordsworth is much less accommodating of the new sciences than at first appears. He is much less hopeful than he sounds that this time will ever come. And we may hear in those phrases 'flesh and blood' and 'dear and genuine inmate of the household of Man' echoes of the long and cold repose into which Blake's Albion had sunk. The sciences have no human warmth, they do not resonate with our hearts, they are, in short, not genuine housemates. They do not belong. Wordsworth may be disingenuous here, deliberately misleading when he implies an accommodation and cooperation between poetry and science of which he had not the slightest expectation.

But then we remember the quite different approach to the new sciences on the Continent, of which Wordsworth himself knew directly, and through Coleridge. Those approaches may have offered a realistic chance of a rapprochement between poetry and science where little in England did.

And we know that Wordsworth appreciated these issues from a line in another early poem: 'We murder to dissect.' Better, I suppose, if we murder and then dissect. It is the murdering as we dissect that is most troubling. It is true that earlier in this same poem Words-

30

worth rejects all book learning, the arts as well as the sciences and not just anatomical studies. Such learning is irrelevant compared to the insight we gain from walking through a wood in spring-time. So Wordsworth's critique of the new science does not arise, as Blake's does, from confronting the new science with the absolute authority of intellection, inspiration, imagination, and faith in the Saviour. Wordsworth's critique proceeds from the view that the new science can accommodate nothing of the living which is lived in the world around us, whether complex or rudimentary.

As an argument against the new science, this insistence on the importance of sensation has advantages over Blake's approach. For everyone has some sense of the liveliness of the creatures around us, while only a few understand the centrality of intellection. Again, Wordsworth's argument attacks the sciences on their own ground, where the argument from intellection introduces entirely different considerations. How well Wordsworth understood intellection and could display it to us, we have discussed with the *Ode*. But it is not from this point of view that he approaches the new sciences.

Still, it may be that this difference between Blake and Wordsworth is less than it appears. Wordsworth celebrates life in all the forms around him. This is the dimension of the created order which concerns him. And he is ideally placed for this celebration since he thinks that the human mind is perfectly adjusted to the natural creation and reveals its greatest beauties. Consciousness is the spirit of the creation and creation serves consciousness. The physical universe is primarily how souls experience, and the intellection of Being is the source and goal of all. Wordsworth's insistence on the creation as sensory is a corollary of the view he and Blake both held, that we and our world are primarily spiritual not material.

This carrying of sensation into the midst of the objects studied is the purpose of another early poem. Here the sensation at issue is the feeling of pleasure or enjoyment:

> *Lines Written in Early Spring*
> I heard a thousand blended notes,
> While in a grove I sate reclined,

In that sweet mood when pleasant thoughts
Bring sad thoughts to the mind.

To her fair works did nature link
The human soul that through me ran:
And much it grieved my heart to think
What man has made of man.

Through primrose-tufts, in that sweet bower,
The periwinkle trailed its wreathes;
And 'tis my faith that every flower
Enjoys the air it breathes.

The birds around me hopped and played:
Their thoughts I cannot measure,
But the least motion which they made,
It seemed a thrill of pleasure.

The budding twigs spread out their fan,
To catch the breezy air;
And I must think, do all I can,
That there was pleasure there.

If this belief from heaven be sent,
If such be nature's holy plan,
Have I not reason to lament
What man has made of man?[3]

In the third, fourth and fifth stanzas Wordsworth attributes feelings
of pleasure to flowers, birds and the twigs of trees. But though he is
confident that these creatures do, indeed, enjoy themselves, he asks
himself how he knows this. So in the third verse it is his faith that
flowers enjoy the air they breathe; in the fourth the motions of the
birds seem to him thrills of pleasure; and in the fifth verse he supposes that the twigs feel pleasure though he does his best not to suppose it. He is forced to believe it. In the last verse he suggests that
the belief that these creatures enjoy themselves is sent from Heaven
and is part of the sacred design of the Creation.

Why is he struck by how he knows these things? Because other
people have questioned this and this makes him sad. He laments

3. Ibid, p. 377.

what man has made of man when they refuse to acknowledge the joy in the creatures around them. Who refuses to acknowledge this? We have already introduced Descartes and the vivisectionists and they may be whom he has in mind. Or perhaps Wordsworth is not thinking of philosophers at all but of our common human propensity to fail to notice the world around us. But this, I think, is less likely. Wordsworth is actively working here at seeing the world without this enjoying of itself. He is not concerned with mere inadvertence. Again, he tells us that he cannot measure the thoughts of birds, as though only quantifiable evidence will count in this argument.

This is a philosophical issue, and it arises when we ask how we know what we know about other minds and sentient beings. It is a philosophical issue because it is discussed by people who are commonly called philosophers. Consider the following passage from Wittgenstein's *Philosophical Investigations*:

> Say to yourself, for example: "The children over there are mere automata; all their liveliness is mere automatism." And you will either find these words becoming quite empty; or you will produce in yourself some kind of uncanny feeling, or something of that sort.[4]

Wittgenstein is talking of children here, not plants or birds, but his discomfort is comparable to Wordsworth's lament. Something sinister happens when we ask these questions, and when we attempt to justify our belief in the minds and feelings of others. And again it is to Descartes that we trace this peculiarly solipsistic procedure. Each of us can be sure only of 'I think, therefore I am.' Each must therefore derive from that a belief in the existence of everything else. Wordsworth's poem here is a counter meditation to Descartes'. And, of course, Descartes' uncertain inferences did not take him very far, since he did not suppose even animals conscious.

Wordsworth himself gives us all he is going to give us of his theory in the second verse:

---

4. Wittgenstein, L., *Philosophical Investigations*, trs: Anscombe, Hacker, Schulte, 2009, Wiley Blackwell, p. 133.

> To her fair works did Nature link
> The human soul that through me ran:

This is ambiguous as to where the human soul ran. Does Wordsworth mean that the soul which is all through him and stops at his surface is linked to the works of Nature? Or does he mean that the soul which runs through him runs beyond him also, into other works of Nature? There is evidence for the second of these readings when we compare this couplet to a climactic passage in *Tintern Abbey*:

> And I have felt
> A presence that disturbs me with the joy
> Of elevated thoughts; a sense sublime
> Of something far more deeply interfused,
> Whose dwelling is the light of setting suns,
> And the round ocean, and the living air,
> And the blue sky, and in the mind of man,
> A motion and a spirit, that impels
> All thinking things, all objects of all thought,
> And rolls through all things.[5]

The motion and spirit which rolls through all things rolls through Wordsworth too. What he remembered above the banks of the Wye was the joyful sense of how that universal spirit brings the whole of the creation into a single consciousness, the ocean and the living air as well as all thinking things. The metaphor of his soul's running through him is the rolling through all things by that single spirit.

In his account of the vision in *Tintern Abbey* Wordsworth introduces an element which we have not seen in the two images of eternity in the *Intimations Ode*. It is the notion of universal inclusivity. Neither with the Being of the eternal silence nor with the immortal sea are we made aware of how everything in the living world is united in this state of elevation. *Tintern Abbey* is earlier than the *Intimations Ode*, and the account of vision in the earlier poem is comparatively rhetorical in its several repetitions of the word 'all.' It is grandiloquent. But in this passage as in those later ones, the

5. Wordsworth, op. cit., p. 163.

language describing the absolute is simple and quite untheological. A presence, a motion and a spirit, these are very chaste and modest words. As for carrying sensation into the midst of the objects of the science itself, 'the living air' does it in a phrase.

But the materialist may say that Wordsworth is less inclusive than he thinks. He has, it seems, two categories: the first is all thinking things and the second is all objects of all thought. But these two categories by no means exhaust reality, since there is also the category of objects which are not thought by any thinking thing. And this category is much larger than the other two put together. We may, of course, say to this that this third category is now an object of our thought, though it is by definition very vague. But the point is an important one, and it gives some force to Keats' characterization of Wordsworthian vision as the egotistical sublime. Keats' comment gains special force from Keats' himself achieving the same vision in the *Ode to Psyche*. He knows as well as Wordsworth what that sublimity is.

The ideal inclusivity of Wordsworth's vision in *Tintern Abbey* is one aspect of the *totum simul*, which is the object and subject of the intellectual act. It is a different aspect of the *totum simul* from the one we have seen with Blake. Blake saw the present, past and future all at once before him. Wordsworth sees the whole of animated nature and the being which interfuses and unites it. But each of them experiences an elevation from which they are aware of a stupendous unitary reality. In Wordsworth's case it is a direct apprehension of the single enjoying and suffering spirit which pervades the world. His capacity to feel it is at once disturbing and joyful. It is disturbing because so joyful.

We began with the *Ode* and Wordsworth's accounts of intellection there, the eternal silence and the immortal sea. We noted how the *Ode* was timeless, and could have been written in almost any period. To see what Wordsworth thought of the new sciences, we went to the *Preface* and the lines written in early spring. Wordsworth here did not confront the new thinking with the fact of intellection or inspiration as Blake did. Instead he advanced certain reservations concerning its capacity to see the life in the objects of its study. The new science is remote, and its sympathies are not wide like the poet's, not the common property of humankind. That is why the poet is needed by the scientists' side, to make us all feel the living wonders which the scientist studies. But with the lines from *Tintern Abbey* we understand that this capacity to feel the living experience of other creatures, however we come by it, is the foundation and principle of his intellection on certain occasions. It is the opening by which he is transported to a much larger state of being, and it is the form which that selfless self-expansion takes. The new science as practised is ignorant of this, and the poet must await the time when scientists see the life in things again.

We may detect a distinct philosophic development from the earlier pantheism of *Tintern Abbey* to the Platonic recollections and visions of the later *Ode*. To the argument of this essay this does not matter very much, since both poems display intellection. Neither discusses the scientific world view or the historical context. There is a discretion in Wordsworth's dealing with the new sciences, but his deliberate distance from them in the *Preface* and his lament for a humanity disconnected from the world's enjoyment in the *Spring* poem indicate his feelings. Unlike Blake he is not troubled much by how the new sciences destroy the 'wisdom of ages.' But the empiricism which insists that what we know we learn from our senses only, breaks a kind of compact with Heaven, in Wordsworth's view, and imposes a boundary on ourselves which quite precludes the spirit.

3

Samuel Taylor Coleridge

We have offended, Oh! My countrymen!
We have offended very grievously,
And been most tyrannous. From east to west
A groan of accusation pierces Heaven!
The wretched plead against us; multitudes
Countless and vehement, the sons of God,
Our brethren! Like a cloud that travels on,
Steamed up from Cairo's swamps of pestilence,
Even so, my countrymen! have we gone forth
And borne to distant tribes slavery and pangs,
And, deadlier far, our vices, whose deep taint
With slow perdition murders the whole man,
His body and his soul! Meanwhile, at home,
All individual dignity and power
Engulfed in Courts, Committees, Institutions,
Associations and Societies,
A vain, speech-mouthing, speech-reporting Guild,
One Benefit-Club for mutual flattery.
We have drunk up, demure as at a grace,
Pollutions from the brimming cup of wealth.[1]

T HIS IS THE COLERIDGE we recognize in Hazlitt's account of
him in 1798, the same year as the poem. Hazlitt heard him
preach on war and it was a revelation. But where Blake read
England's conquests as the deliberate occlusion of every other
nation's spiritual life, Coleridge saw England as driven by greed.

---

1. Coleridge, S. T., 'Fears in Solitude', *Selected Poetry and Prose of Coleridge*, 1951, USA, Random House Inc., pp. 65–66.

Blake saw the energizing force of England's expansion as envy and the desire to destroy the wisdom of ages. Coleridge saw that force as the desire for material satisfactions, which had usurped other essential needs of his society. But they were at one in their sense of the peculiar new relations between the members of the imperialist class. Coleridge described how all individual responsibility had disappeared into committees, while Blake described how all the males had conjoined into one male and then each became a ravening cancer.

In a later essay in *The Friend*, Coleridge goes much further.[2] The desire for material satisfactions is the reason for trade between individuals and nations, and this is as essential a human function as any. But it is not the only desire in people. The desire for spiritual fulfilment is the reason for literature which is also exchanged between individuals and nations, and these two human activities, trade and literature, constitute the two major bonds among human kind. For Coleridge, the richest discovery to be made in the study of history is this: that in a society where literature predominates over trade, trade will flourish to the fullest desirable extent; but where trade dominates over literature, that society will eventually collapse. But this is a truth, he writes, which a wealthy and commercial nation is most unwilling to hear. For Coleridge, then, the course of history is the oscillation between periods in which literature predominates and periods in which trade does. But the periods in which trade dominates are comparatively short-lived. It is noticeable that Coleridge's philosophy of history, as he calls it, is not progressive like Hegel's which was contemporary with it.

As for Coleridge's term 'literature', it means primarily scripture, the words of the inspired prophets among the world's peoples. Coleridge supposes them all to be in search of a single principle, around the globe and through all history. They are seeking the principle from which the physical universe on the one hand, and human consciousness on the other, both emerged. In this search the common impulse is to rush out into the natural world to try to find the sources of our human experience there. But this is to make the mis-

2. Coleridge, S.T., *The Friend*, Section II, Essay II, Books for Libraries Press, New York, 1867, pp. 335–345.

take of Narcissus who fell in love with his own reflection without ever realizing that it was his reflection. The materialist supposes physical Nature to be the origin of our experience, without ever realizing that Nature is as it is for us because of what we bring to it. And here Coleridge reprises the fundamental insights of Plato and Kant, that our world of experience is informed by a range of understandings which cannot be derived from our experience of the world. For we could experience no world without them. The crude empiricism of Locke and Hume must yield to a more sophisticated analysis of those logical preconditions which enable human experience.

So, as far as science goes, the inward logical enquiry is necessarily prior to the outward search in Nature. The Kantian synthetic *a priori* which enable our conception of time, space and causation are much more inclusive than are Plato's mathematical ideas. But Kant must yield to Plato in one vital respect, according to Coleridge. Plato supposed that the mathematical ideas could be apprehended directly without any representation. For Plato this was the difference between intellection, which made no use of representations, and the mathematical sciences which used them. But Kant supposed that there could be no such direct intellection. Here Coleridge was with Plato and against Kant. But Coleridge was always more given to seeing similarities than differences. He thought that Bacon, Blake's monster, was also a thorough Platonist in this respect who believed that beyond the various idols of our misunderstanding, there were the real forms of nature waiting to be discovered.

From this point Coleridge makes a great leap. Having established that Nature and its laws are the products of our consciousness in these ways, the essay proceeds to a kind of rapture:

> Hast thou ever raised thy mind to the consideration of EXISTENCE, in and by itself, as the mere act of existing? Hast thou ever said to thyself thoughtfully, IT IS! heedless in that moment, whether it were a man before thee, or a flower, or a grain of sand? Without reference, in short, to this or that particular mode or form of existence? If thou hast indeed attained to this, thou wilt have felt the presence of a mystery, which must have fixed thy spirit in awe and wonder. The very words, There is nothing! or There was a time, when there was nothing! are self-contradictory.

There is that within us which repels the proposition with as full and instantaneous light, as if it bore evidence against the fact in the right of its own eternity.

Not TO BE, then, is impossible: TO BE, incomprehensible. If thou hast mastered this intuition of absolute existence, thou will have learnt likewise, that it was this, and no other, which in the earlier ages seized the nobler minds, the elect among men, with a sort of sacred horror. This it was which first caused them to feel within themselves a something ineffably greater than their own individual nature. It was this which, raising them aloft, and projecting them to an ideal distance from themselves, prepared them to become the lights and awakening voices of other men, the founders of law and religion, the educators and foster-gods of mankind.

Coleridge moves here from the not uncommon experience of saying thoughtfully about something to oneself 'It is' to the sacred horror of the nobler minds in earlier ages. A point between these two may be the recognition that this being gripped by the bare existence of a thing has helped the prophets of the past to their wisdom. This thoughtfulness is the opening of the door into that wisdom. Having engaged our agreement to the simple saying 'It is,' Coleridge picks us up and takes us straight into a vision.

His vision of Being is a long leap either from the Kantian and Platonic presuppositions which enable our experiences of time, space and causality, or from saying of something 'It is.' The experience of time, space and causality is general among humans, while to say 'It is' of something is common. But Coleridge's vision of Being is confined to the noblest minds only. This is where the Platonic and Kantian self-consciousness is crucial. For to realize just how our minds shape our sensory experience is to have begun that movement from the outer to the inner world which culminates in the intellection of Being. German thought is philosophical here while British empiricism is the flat denial of philosophy's power to transform us.

For Coleridge, as for Blake and Wordsworth, a concomitant of intellection is a yielding of the individual self-hood:

It is absolutely one, and that it is, and affirms itself TO BE, is its only predicate. And yet this power, nevertheless, is! In eminence of

Being it IS! And he for whom it manifests itself in its adequate idea, dare as little arrogate it to himself as his own, can as little appropriate it either totally or by partition, as he can claim ownership in the breathing air, or make an enclosure in the cope of heaven. He bears witness of it to his own mind, even as he describes life and light: and, with the silence of light, it describes itself and dwells in *us* only as far as we dwell in *it*.

Coleridge has much in common with Blake, in his hatred of England's adventures overseas, and again in this loss of self in the supreme act of intellection. But there is one respect in which Coleridge is much more like Wordsworth than like Blake. And that is in his use of a quite secular language for his spiritual writing where Blake draws directly on the terms and symbols of Christianity. Not merely Wordsworth's images but his symbols too are taken from the natural world, just as Coleridge here describes the revelations of noble spirits around the globe in a language almost equally distant from them. Here Coleridge is clearly attempting to universalize his insight across humankind. But Wordsworth too envisions the poet as a man speaking to men, helping to bring the whole world into relationship. We may hypothesize that their use of common speech and their avoidance of terms specific to a single tradition were deliberate.

So Coleridge and Wordsworth have this in common with Plato, not only what they say but their manner of saying it. They have discovered or invented an original means of delivering the ancient message about human destiny. We may compare the Homeric teaching with the Platonic, to see how the narrative of the Gods has almost entirely disappeared in Plato. In the same way Coleridge and Wordsworth are no longer Christian though Coleridge was a Unitarian minister. Plato is not yet bound to the systematic use of his terminology but uses the same key words in quite different ways in different contexts. With Aristotle the language hardens into the first formal philosophical vocabulary. Like Plato, Wordsworth and Coleridge are fresh and natural, and find ways of saying the loftiest things in the simplest words.

How well does Coleridge's account fit the very various spiritual traditions around the globe? Here we remember Wordsworth's difficulties concerning the pre-existence of the human soul. If Wordsworth could not co-ordinate the Classical Western and Christian traditions, what chance was there of such a universalist perspective as Coleridge attempts? Do all the world's religions turn on the apprehension of some ultimate being either in a particular object or as *totum simul*? The procedure of this whole essay and my account of intellection in its second paragraph are open to a similar objection. Does my model of intellection really fit even these three Romantics? And how does Coleridge's account square with Taoism, say, or Islam? And we have already excluded the traditions of non-literate peoples. Coleridge makes an heroic generalization at the level of the intellect, and he does it not as a comparative religionist, nor as a cultural anthropologist, but as a visionary and spiritual teacher. This is his response to England's worldwide exploitation. For Blake and Coleridge, England and its bureaucracy are the core of the world's darkness. And it is just because it is English that they can understand it as they do, and can act against it, for they are Englishmen too. So the Chinese, it is said, believe that the herb needed to heal an illness will grow near any who need it.

When Coleridge turns to the relations between his vision of Being and the new sciences, he distinguishes between them in two different ways. Firstly, he tells a story. Imagine, he says, a rude and unlettered African into whose possession there comes a copy of the Holy Bible in his language. He studies this strange object assiduously and eventually determines that all the marks on its many pages belong to a limited number of different kinds. Of course, he will suppose that there are many more such kinds than there are letters in the alphabet, since he will suppose that each capital letter is of a different kind from the same letter in lower case. This, for Coleridge, stands for the state of the new sciences.

But now a friendly missionary arrives, and teaches this African how to read. At last, the book makes sense, not just because he can now read the verses and follow the story, but because there is within the African a recognition of the truth which the Bible tells. His is the state of the philosopher and visionary who has learnt to read Nature aright. And, of course this distinction which Coleridge is making between the philosopher and the new scientist turns on one very obvious assumption, for which Coleridge does not offer the slightest evidence. He assumes that Nature is a language and a book written by God for us to read.

That Coleridge did think this is clear from several poems, such as *Frost at Midnight*:

> But *thou*, my babe! shalt wander like a breeze
> By lakes and sandy shores, beneath the crags
> Of ancient mountain, and beneath the clouds,
> Which image in their bulk both lakes and shores
> And mountain crags: so shalt thou see and hear
> The lovely shapes and sounds intelligible
> Of that eternal language, which thy God
> Utters, who from eternity doth teach
> Himself in all, and all things in himself.
> Great universal Teacher! He shall mould
> Thy spirit, and by giving make it ask.[3]

This belief in Nature as a language is part of the Christian view that God has given us at least two paths to Him, the book of scripture and the book of Nature. So there is all this in Coleridge's account of the unlettered African and his Bible. But are we really to suppose the new science has done no more than count the different elements, forces, plants, animals and so on? So Coleridge thought and he was a man who showed the greatest interest in scientific discovery and experimentation. He was a close friend of Humphry Davy and Joseph Banks. Here we must remember that we are not talking of the material exploitation of scientific discoveries, but only of the knowledge which they offer of the world. Coleridge makes a good point for our time as for his. Indeed, our science still leads us endlessly on through atoms, subatomic particles, quantum physics, string theory etc., etc. Our case at the end is much worse than the African's who had indeed managed to determine the actual number of different kinds of marks before him. For us the endless labyrinth of the physicists' possibilities opens and ever opens into more.

The second way in which Coleridge distinguishes between his vision of knowledge and the new sciences is more epistemological:

---

3. Op. cit., 'Frost at Midnight,' *Selected Poetry and Prose*, p. 4.

The ground-work, therefore, of all true philosophy is the full apprehension of the difference between the contemplation of reason, namely, that intuition of things which arises when we possess ourselves, as one with the whole, which is substantial knowledge, and that which presents itself when transferring reality to the negations of reality, to the ever-varying framework of the uniform life, we think of ourselves as separated beings, and place nature in antithesis to the mind, as object to subject, thing to thought, death to life. This is abstract knowledge, or the science of the mere understanding. By the former, we know that existence is its own predicate, self-affirmation, the one attribute in which all others are contained, not as parts, but as manifestations. It is an eternal and infinite self-rejoicing, self-loving, with a joy unfathomable, with a love all comprehensive. It is absolute; and the absolute is neither singly that which affirms, nor that which is affirmed; but the identity and living copula of both.

On the other hand, the abstract knowledge which belongs to us as finite beings, and which leads to a science of delusion then only, when it would exist for itself instead of being the instrument of the former—instead of being, as it were, a translation of the living word into a dead language, for the purposes of memory, arrangement, and general communication—it is by this abstract knowledge that the understanding distinguishes the affirmed from the affirming. Well if it distinguish without dividing! Well! if by distinction it add clearness to fulness, and prepare for the intellectual re-union of the all in one, in that eternal reason whose fulness hath no opacity, whose transparency hath no vacuum.

Though this is analytical in method, it follows on from the Bible story in its account of abstract knowledge or the science of the mere understanding. This science studies the ever-varying framework of the uniform life for the purpose of memory, arrangement and general communication. It is a painstaking taxonomical exercise after the manner of the unlettered African. And that is all it is, since Coleridge is not in the least concerned with the powers which any science may give us in the physical world. He is concerned only with the knowledge it gives. And that being so, this abstract knowledge is entirely secondary to intellection, which Coleridge calls here the contemplation of reason. We can catch here more than an echo of those great German philosophers of science from Leibniz to Karl von Humboldt who actually organized learned academies on the basis Coleridge describes. The guiding principle is the subordination of the physical sciences to the more purely intellectual.

Coleridge is very well aware that abstract knowledge, the mere understanding, can disrupt the contemplation of reason. In his last two sentences he gives due warning that the new sciences may obscure Being and distract us from intellection. This may describe the effect of Locke, but it does not describe what David Hume did. Hume, like Bertrand Russell and A. J. Ayer nearer our time, turned upon the very notion of intellection itself and the possibility of divine vision. And here we have to say that Blake had the clearer view. Blake believed that the new science was devised against the wisdom of ages deliberately to destroy it. It does not count much against this view that there are many scientists who are religious. Coleridge is with them here, or too polite to recognize the rift which Blake saw as the future. This rift did not arise from a too zealous enthusiasm for a subordinate study. There was a direct attack on the very possibility of wisdom. To Coleridge the relations between the contemplation of reason and abstract knowledge mirror the relations between literature and trade. In each pair, the second serves the first. If it does not do so, it brings trouble.

Coleridge's account of intellection as the contemplation of reason is the fullest statement so far of the theory with which this essay began. He goes some way here beyond the distinction he made in the story of the unlettered African. The contemplation of reason differs from the mere abstract understanding because in the contemplation of reason there is no distinction between subject and object, while the abstract understanding is precisely what discriminates between subject and object. One precursor of Coleridge's argument here is Aristotle who supposed that the supreme human pleasure was the 'thinking of thinking.' On Aristotle's view the contemplation by the thinker of their thinking is the most inviolable of pleasures just because the object enjoyed is inseparable from the enjoying subject.[4] Since Coleridge, Yeats has described it:

---

4. Aristotle, *Nicomachean Ethics*, Book x.

Such fullness in that quarter overflows
And falls into the basin of the mind
That man is stricken deaf and dumb and blind,
For intellect no longer knows
Is from the ought or knower from the known
That is to say, ascends to Heaven...[5]

The abstract understanding knows nothing of this, since its function is quite different. It assumes the world of experience as a given. It assumes that there is subject in relation to object, thought to thing, life to death. The last pair here is drastic, and reminds us of Wordsworth's remarks concerning the scientists and the carrying of sensation into the midst of the objects of science themselves. But Coleridge is saying that this deadening experience of mere things is also essential since it is the condition under which we can proceed to the numeration and classification of the world's varieties. And in this way we can develop our understanding of Being in its fulness for when the time comes, and we take them all up into ourselves or are, like Wordsworth, completely penetrated by them. But we may question whether this deadening is really necessary to the operations of taxonomy.

In this way, then, Coleridge gives more ground to the new sciences than do Blake and Wordsworth. But the science to which Coleridge grants a role does not, on his account of it, sound very new. The taxonomic organization of the natural world goes back at least to Aristotle and Plato, who had not only mastered the method but the theory which enabled it. What greater worth, if any, did Coleridge see in the work of Harvey, Newton, Boyle? Did he understand that Europe at least had entered a decidedly different phase, as Blake understood this? Coleridge knew Bacon's work as well as Blake did, but he does not seem to have taken fright in the same way. He compares the crude fact-hunting materialist to his unlettered African before the missionary's arrival, but he seems to anticipate no great evil from the new sciences either at home or abroad. He is confident, I think, that they will always be subordinate to the contemplation of reason.

5. Yeats, W.B., *A Dialogue of Self and Soul.*

AMERICA

4

Ralph Waldo Emerson

Give me truths;
For I am weary of the surfaces,
And die of inanition. If I knew
Only the herbs and simples of the wood,
Rue, cinquefoil, gill, vervain and agrimony,
Blue-vetch and trillium, hawkweed, sassafras,
Milkweeds and murky brakes, quaint pipes and sundew,
And rare and virtuous roots, which in these woods
Draw untold juices from the common earth,
Untold, unknown, and I could surely spell
Their fragrance, and their chemistry apply
By sweet affinities to human flesh,
Driving the foe and stablishing the friend, —
O, that were much, and I could be a part
Of the round day, related to the sun
And planted world, and full executor
Of their imperfect functions.
But these young scholars, who invade our hills,
Bold as the engineer who fells the wood,
And travelling often in the cut he makes,
Love not the flower they pluck, and know it not
And all their botany is Latin names.
The old men studied magic in the flowers,
And human fortunes in astronomy,
And an omnipotence in chemistry,
Preferring things to names, for these were men,
Were unitarians of the united world,
And, wheresoever their clear eye-beams fell,
They caught the footsteps of the SAME. Our eyes
Are armed, but we are strangers to the stars,

And strangers to the mystic beast and bird,
And strangers to the plant and to the mine.
The injured elements say, 'Not in us';
And haughtily return us stare for stare.
For we invade them impiously for gain;
We devastate them unreligiously,
And coldly ask their pottage, not their love.
Therefore they shove us from them, yield to us
Only what to our griping toil is due;
But the sweet affluence of love and song,
The rich results of the divine consents
Of man and earth, or world beloved and lover,
The nectar and ambrosia, are withheld;
And in the midst of spoils and slaves, we thieves
And pirates of the universe, shut out
Daily to a more thin and outward rind,
Turn pale and starve. Therefore, to our sick eyes,
The stunted trees look sick, the summer short,
Clouds shade the sun, which will not tan our hay,
And nothing thrives to reach its natural term;
And life, shorn of its venerable length,
Even at its greatest space is a defeat,
And dies in anger that it was a dupe;
And, in its highest noon and wantonness,
Is early frugal, like a beggar's child;
Even in the hot pursuit of the best aims
And prizes of ambition, checks its hand,
Like Alpine cataracts frozen as they leaped,
Chilled with a miserly comparison
Of the toy's purchase with the length of life.[1]

F OR ALL ITS GENTLE TONE, this poem *Blight* is extremely and deliberately provocative. A Harvard graduate in the middle of the 19th century is strenuously arguing for astrology, alchemy,

1. Emerson, Ralph Waldo. Ed: Geoffrey Moore, *The Penguin Book of American Verse*, 1977, England, pp. 78–80.

magic and the medieval bestiaries. Emerson believes these superstitions a much surer foundation for science than are the botany of Linnaeus or the physics of Newton. He even seems to dismiss any increase in human longevity of modern times as inferior to what he calls a 'venerable old age', as though there was no longer respect for old people. He supposes that the natural world had become merely an exploitable factor in an economic equation.

It is just here that the word 'Romantic' acquires its pejorative and deprecating tone. It is a yearning for the unachievable, a nostalgia for what never existed. An idea or a fancy, it is neither historical nor scientifically relevant. On this view Emerson was making the old mistake of supposing that some other age of happy folk-belief was only then sinking out of sight as he wrote. Bishop Corbett made the same mistake in the middle of the 17th century when he sang how the fairies had left England for Ireland and the West Country during the reigns of Elizabeth and then James. In one of Chaucer's tales from the 14th century, the friars are said to have driven the fairies away by hunting through the bushes for illicit love-making. As for the Greeks and Romans, they never seemed actually to see their dryads and nature-spirits. They believed they were there because their ancient poets told them they had been. And even those ancient poets were describing still more ancient times than their own. From this point of view, Emerson's Romanticism is a very widespread error.

And what exactly is Emerson's point when he claims that unlike the moderns, the men of old were unitarians of a united world. How did a scientific pharmacopoeia of the mid 19th century compare with the old herbals? Is not the modern pharmacopeia the same thing on a much grander and more systematic scale? As for the Latin names, they too are part of this universalization, as Latin had been the *lingua franca* of Medieval and Renaissance Europe. The common names of the herbs are by no means uniform, and often confusing. Again, if astrology purported to read human destinies in the stars, Newton had shown how one and the same force held the planets in their courses and moved the tides. It was also a principle in the science of ballistics. Organic chemistry was showing what alchemy never could: how the human body and all living things are carbon-based. So how exactly were Emerson's men of old so much more Unitarian? Their unities were even more partial than those of Emerson's moderns, and they lacked any foundation.

These arguments would not persuade Emerson. They would harden his heart still further against modernity. They typify what he rejects. The mind which thinks and argues like this is exactly the problem for Emerson who sees no understanding here at all. For Emerson, the young scholar, the modern scientist, is like someone who lives in a house in a city without knowing anything about the neighbors or anyone else within ten miles, and who has never walked round the block. But inside the house are all the encyclopaedias you could wish and an hourly communication of intelligence from the four quarters. This is the condition of the young scholars. Though they have come among Emerson's hills, they know only words, not things. Their world is in their heads. Though they have made a serious study of botany and are actually in the field, they are still absent. How much more absent, then, is someone who is not a scientist but suffers from this same scientistic mentality? It is paradoxical that a general acceptance of the empirical method should have left so many people abstracted.

This, then, is the basis of Emerson's peculiar Unitarianism, a lived experience of things. But this experience does not make his system anthropocentric. The old men's herbals deal as much with the treatment of animals. It was also a veterinary pharmacopoeia. The stars which relayed the astrological destinies of human beings were quite as much coordinated with the plants and metals, and so the plants and metals were coordinated with each other astrologically. In the older chemistry of alchemy, it is true, the transmutation of the metals had a profoundly human dimension, where lead symbolized the unregenerate soul and gold its full spiritual realization. But even that was as much about the divine as the human. As for Emerson's mystic bird and beast, they too were symbols of divine human virtues and beastly human vices, and we may perhaps catch an echo of indigenous totemism. The point is that all these understandings connected people to things and thing to thing, across all the levels and orders of our sciences, psychological and physical. But this cannot be said of gravitational force or the varieties of carbon compounds. They operate exclusively, each in its own field, and the relation between those dimensions is obscure.

But by this stage in the argument, the young scholars are growing restive. They demand that Emerson produce his evidence for his astrology, alchemy and bestiary. What are his grounds for believing in these old men's tales? But these tales are not scientific hypotheses at all and were never intended to be. It is the greatest of all scientistic delusions to suppose that people were always striving for the scientific understanding which we have now, and that we alone have succeeded. The old men's Unitarianism was in no way a thesis to be argued but an entry into the living and feeling core of a creature which they knew intimately. The old men's world was an entirely different order of experience from the Academy and its ways of knowing. What is uncanny about the young scholars is that they seem to have no sense of this, then or now. Fifty years before Emerson wrote, Wordsworth had described in much more detail the spiritual deformities of just such a young scholar. I give the passage from *The Prelude* in its final version:

> A miracle of scientific lore,
> Ships he can guide across the pathless sea,
> And tell you all their cunning; he can read
> The inside of the earth, and spell the stars;
> He knows the policies of foreign lands;
> Can string you names of districts, cities, towns,
> The whole world over, tight as beads of dew
> Upon a gossamer thread; he sifts, he weighs;
> All things are put to question; he must live
> Knowing that he grows wiser every day
> Or else not live at all, and seeing too
> Each little drop of wisdom as it falls
> Into the dimpling cistern of his heart:
> For this unnatural growth the trainer blame,
> Pity the tree.—Poor human vanity,
> Wert thou extinguished, little would be left
> Which he could truly love; but how escape?
> For, ever as a thought of purer birth
> Rises to lead him toward a better clime,
> Some intermeddler still is on his watch

To drive him back, and pound him, like a stray,
Within the pinfold of his own conceit.
Meanwhile old granddame earth is grieved to find
The playthings, which her love designed for him,
Unthought of: in their woodland beds the flowers
Weep, and the river sides are all forlorn.[2]

This is a deeply unpleasant mentality. Emerson shows another side of its arrogance. A family of farmers for generations in the same place, a hunter, a wise woman and her herbs, do these people know nothing? Does their far greater experience of the plants, stars and animals around them not outweigh the new simplistic sciences? Compared to that folk-knowledge, the insights afforded by the laboratory and observatory seem superficial. And how many of us have examined such creatures there? How apt is the scientific thesis or the learned book on natural science as a vehicle for revealing truths about the natural world? The form of such works unfits them for nature. There is nothing in the world as unmusical as a scientific thesis.

Emerson remarks that the young scholars use Latin names for the plants, instead of the homely names he has just listed. Why does this not please him as a return to the ways of the men of old? But this Latinization is part of the problem as he sees it. Why should we say 'vervaine' rather than 'verbena'? Why his strong preference for the folk-names? Consider the old word 'womb' and then consider the experience of a woman whose doctor tells her that she has a disease of the uterus. It is part of medical cant to call the womb the uterus and the use of the Latin word here conveys a professional authority. But what if the word 'womb' more or less drops out of the language, replaced by 'uterus'? It is as though we have become clinical about our own bodies. We look at them in the same terms as the doctor considers a patient. We have made objects of ourselves. The process is even clearer with the cant of psychology. 'Depression' is a clinical term and there are certain objective criteria which establish its presence. These criteria include the subjects' description of themselves as sad. So, typically, the word 'depressed' should be used of a second or third person but not oneself unless under clinical observation.

2. Wordsworth, William, op. cit., *Poetical Works*, p. 525.

The case is still clearer with the word 'aggression.' I am angry but you and she are experiencing feelings of aggression. These cant terms have become popular to the point where 'I am depressed' sounds all right but 'I am aggressive' does not quite yet. This move is always towards an objectification of the subject, the replacing of first-person language with third-person language, and both 'depression' and 'aggression' are Latinate.

The bleeding of the professional and professorial language of botany into the colloquial is in itself an estrangement, in addition to the loss of the old, direct herbal knowledge. The young scholars with their Latin terms are aliens with a foreign tongue who have invaded Emerson's hills. They are different and their Latinisms impose on him. The common names of the flowers and stars yield to a scientific nomenclature which ignores his intimacy with these as 'dear and familiar inmates of the household of man.' The things are set apart, but we are the ones reduced. The young scholars' arrival is a physical irruption into an ordered human universe within a specific locale. The intellectual ordering of that world before the invasion depended, as it should, on an immediate knowledge of the stars, plants and animals found in that locale. Without that immediate knowledge, most of what we now call science is hearsay and second-hand. Blake makes the same point:

> And every Space that a Man views around his dwelling-place
> Standing on his own roof or in his garden on a mount
> Of twenty-five cubits in height, such space is his Universe:
> And on its verge the Sun rises & sets, the Clouds bow
> To meet the flat Earth & the Sea in such an order'd Space:
> The Starry heavens reach no further, but here bend and set
> On all sides, & the two Poles turn on their valves of gold;
> And if he move his dwelling-place, his heavens also move
> Where'er he goes, & all his neighbourhood bewail his loss.
> Such are the Spaces called Earth & such its dimension.
> As to that false appearance which appears to the reasoner
> As of a Globe rolling thro' Voidness, it is a delusion of Ulro.[3]

Blake's astronomy here is compatible with the principles of astrology but not with the heliocentric hypothesis.

---

3. Blake, op. cit., *K.* 516, *M.* 29–14.

This estrangement from our immediate experience of the flowers and stars is for Emerson the crucial feature of modern thinking. He feels it intensely, and this intense understanding is the climax of the poem. He feels as if the creatures around him are shutting him out and in their repeated 'not in us' the poem momentarily exceeds its quiet, meditative tone to become rhetorical and impassioned. Suddenly the creatures which are physically close to him retreat and reject him. This is the blight which the young scholars bring. We have seen in Wordsworth's description of the flowers and river banks we have deserted how these creatures bewail our departure. Blake, too, supposed that Albion once contained within himself the whole universe. But Albion fell, and the stars and heaven rushed away from him in horror. There is a Jewish tradition that Adam Kadmon contained the whole world within himself but with his exit from the garden, the world deserted him. So Emerson's complaint is not new with the Romantics. No doubt the mentality of the young scholars or of those miracles of scientific lore was common enough at other times. But in our time if not Emerson's, it is for the first time the dominant mentality.

The notion that all the creatures around us cry 'not in us' and repudiate our part in them is what John Ruskin called a pathetic fallacy, a case of attributing human thoughts, feelings and motives to non-human creatures erroneously. But, of course, this is merely what it looks like from the standpoint of the modern mentality. Emerson would not accept that he was in error even in this case. Just as the modern mentality insists that its scientific journals constitute the paradigm of understanding, it insists that the immense distance between researchers in the laboratory and their objects of study is the paradigm of human interaction with the natural world. Research in the field is allowed by extension, but it is necessarily even more dispassionate, and as distant as it can arrange. The notion that we are somehow all mixed up with the other creatures by intuition and empathy may even be true, hypothetically, in certain cases, but it cannot be assumed. For the purpose of the new science, we should think of ourselves as Martians, aliens on another planet quite unlike our own.

But our eternity is a human eternity, Novalis said. When I see a tree, somewhere in here I imagine myself standing there with many arms. Dogs see humans as dogs, and humans see dogs as humans. That is how it is with creatures. Xenophanes said that if cows and horses worshipped Gods, they would think of them as cows and horses. I am grateful to Xenophanes for his suggestion these animals may worship. But whether animals worship divinities of their own kinds or the newborn Zeus or Jesus, I leave open. The fairies realized humanity in the non-human world, and the dwarf-god of the mines is often impossible to distinguish from a human miner. In antiquity, the nymphs humanized trees, rivers, mountains and seas, and Wordsworth exclaimed how he would give up his hope of salvation in Christ to see Proteus or Triton in the ocean before him.

We entertain the fond belief that nature is entirely indifferent to our attitude to it unless we disturb the ecological balance. We think Emerson's description of how it shuts us out is a metaphor, transferring our shutting it out to its shutting us out. But Nature may be far more tolerant of physical abuse than it is of human contempt. What if Emerson were right and the natural world itself, and insofar as it is conscious, has turned away from us? The new science with its laboratory techniques and its freezing dispassion has changed nature, which has responded by solidifying and becoming more opaque. One clear difference between the medieval and modern worlds is miracle, in which the natural world conforms to the needs of the spirit in the human world. As this becomes less imaginable in the human world, so the natural world retreats to mere physical causation. But, as Blake said, all natural effects have spiritual causes, and natural causes merely seem.

The so-called 'increase ceremonies' of Harvest Thanksgiving or the Rain Dance are not a pathetically feeble protoscience. They do not manipulate the natural world so that it will produce for farmers or hunters. They were not a ludicrous precursor of superphosphates and agribusiness. As Wittgenstein pointed out, these ceremonies occur during or after the season and not before it. They are ways of getting alongside the natural rhythms and they may well be essential to the order of things. The fact that these ceremonies have largely disappeared in the Anglosphere without any apparent response from the non-human world is little comfort. The reserves of grace laid up by centuries of devoted worship may still be carrying us. Traditionally, humanity is the priesthood of the natural order and Nature worships through us. When the human link between nature and the divine is broken, who knows what happens? I do not think Emerson is poetic and metaphorical in his account of nature's new resistance to us.

After our repeatedly being rejected by all the other creatures, Emerson introduces a new explanation for the rejection, our impious and unreligious invasion of nature for gain. Unlike the old men, what we take from nature now is theft, not gift. We are thieves and pirates of the universe and, in the last line, misers. Like Esau in the Bible, we give up our birthright for a mess of pottage. And so we gain only what is due to our griping toil. This last phrase is provocative. Such toil, we are taught, was the mean subsistence living of the feudal peasant, but Emerson sees it as true of the moderns, not our ancestors.

Before he describes how nature rejects us, Emerson attributes the rejection to the loss of the old men's knowledge and the arrival of the young scholars with their Latinized botany. After describing the rejection, Emerson attributes it to the impious seeking of gain. What is the relation of the new sciences to seeking gain? The young scholars may not love the flowers, but do they seek wealth? Coleridge, as we have seen, supposes the British geopolitical expansion to be driven by greed. Blake, on the other hand, saw it as a deliberate program to destroy spiritual vision in humanity world-wide. Emerson knew Coleridge's work and had read *The Friend* in which, as we have seen, Coleridge seems to associate the new sciences with trade rather than with literature. Still more likely, Emerson here was influenced by Thomas Taylor, and by Taylor's footnote to his translation of Plotinus, *Concerning the Beautiful*:

> On all sides, nothing of philosophy remains but the name, and this is become the subject of the vilest prostitution: since it is not only engrossed by the Naturalist, Chemist and Anatomist, but is usurped by the Mechanic, in every trifling invention, and made subservient to the lucre of traffic and merchandize. There cannot surely be a greater proof of the degeneracy of the times than so unparalleled a degradation and so barbarous a perversion of terms.

Thomas Taylor was the most influential translator of Plato for Emerson and the Americans.[4] Through Taylor Emerson came to know his band of grandees: Homer, Heraclitus, Empedocles, Plato, Plotinus, Olympiodorus, Proclus, Synesius and the rest, and it is from these and Thomas Taylor that Emerson's theory of nature was developed. Still, Taylor should have remembered from Plato's *Republic* that there too the little bald-headed tinkers had taken over philosophy in late 5th Century Athens, though at least they did not trouble the world with trifling mechanical inventions. And they were more driven by the love of honour than of gain.

Through Taylor, Neoplatonism is a major but subtle influence on Emerson's poem. Despite its simple language and conversational tone, the vision which sustains the poem is that nature is a symbol of the divine and that this is the only possible natural science. Emerson wrote:

> Our science is sensual, and therefore superficial. The earth and the heavenly bodies, physics, and chemistry, we sensually treat, as if they were self-existent; but these are the retinue of that Being we have. "The mighty heaven," said Proclus, "exhibits, in its transfigurations, clear images of the splendour of intellectual perceptions; being moved in conjunction with the unapparent periods of intellectual natures." Therefore, science always goes abreast with the just elevation of the man, keeping step with religion and metaphysics; or, the state of science is the index of our self-knowledge. Since everything in nature answers to a moral power, if any phenomenon remains brute and dark, it is because the corresponding faculty in the observer is not yet active.[5]

By this measure, our science now as then, more now than then, hardly qualifies for the name 'science.' For now all the powers of nature are brute force and randomness. For Emerson this means that almost none of our faculties are active. We are almost without self-knowledge. If, then, natural science always maintains the closest connection with religion and metaphysics as it did in antiquity,

4. *Thomas Taylor the Platonist,* Eds: K. Raine and G. Harper, 1969, Princeton U.P., Princeton, p. 159.
5. Ralph Waldo Emerson, *Essays,* The Spencer Press, 1936, USA, pp. 260–261.

the Middle Ages and the Renaissance, we are very close now to having no natural science at all.

But for Emerson, the Neoplatonist is not the only scientist. The elevation of human beings by science was in his time much more common, and he could see it all around him:

> Who loves nature? Who does not? Is it only poets, and men of leisure and cultivation, who live with her? No; but also hunters, farmers, grooms, and butchers, though they express their affection in their choice of life, and not in their choice of words. The writer wonders what the coachman or the hunter values in riding, in horses, and dogs. It is not superficial qualities. When you talk with him, he holds these at as slight a rate as you. His worship is sympathetic; he has no definitions, but he is commanded in nature, by the living power which he feels to be there present. No imitation, or playing of these things, would content him; he loves the earnest of the north wind, of rain, of stone, and wood, and iron. A beauty not explicable is dearer than a beauty which we can see to the end of. It is nature the symbol, nature certifying the supernatural, body overflowed by life, which he worships, with coarse but sincere rites.[6]

This sounds like Socrates, the man to whom people went for wisdom but heard merely of cobblers and carpenters. Socrates supposed that the carpenter looked to the idea of the bed in order to make a bed. The crafts were necessarily contemplative. Emerson sees his coachmen and groom still bound into nature by love. But we in the early 21st Century have largely lost this too along with the Neoplatonism. So the equation becomes: does our new science equal or surpass the grand spiritual tradition of natural philosophy from Homer to Leibniz PLUS that intimate knowledge of nature and its materials common to traditional workers?

These two excerpts appear on adjacent pages in Emerson's essay *The Poet*. From Proclus to butchers in a page! For the fact is that it is the idealists alone who can penetrate the material with any real understanding. The people whom we now call scientists do not care at all since the laboratory and observatory forbid it. But in their hobbies and sometimes in their faith they return to the human.

6. Op. cit., p. 261.

5

Herman Melville

MELVILLE's *Clarel* is 18,000 lines long, though they are short lines. But we consider here a single, fascinating character who appears only briefly. This character is an American soldier, now serving in one of the armies of the Levant. He is called Ungar.

Ungar is an Amerindian name, and he is a descendent of English Catholic refugees to Maryland, one of whom took an Indian bride. It is significant that he calls himself by an Indian name. Though he is not a Catholic nor attached to any creed, he is deeply sympathetic to the common life of Christendom in the medieval period. But even here he is critical. As he joins Clarel and the other pilgrims at a late stage in their journey through the Holy Land, Ungar knows the landscape intimately by direct acquaintance as well as through scripture.

He had opposed slavery before the Civil War, but he fought in the Confederate army and bore the scars. His reasons for fighting on the Confederate side are not made clear, except by implication. The implication is, I think, that he chose the traditional life of the South, without slavery but otherwise on its own terms. With the Confederate defeat, he had exiled himself from America, and now served as an officer in the Levant. Indeed, he seems to be on some professional business as he joins the pilgrims. He is withdrawn at the beginning and as a fellow-American he intrigues the other pilgrims, so that they seek to draw him out. Ungar is described as a wandering Ishmael of the West, and he has much in common with the narrator of *Moby Dick*. Melville describes him as having no sense of humor, but he does have a biting irony and an acute awareness of how he seems to other people. So it takes some little time before they can provoke him into a candid statement of his views. And all the urging is on their side. But when at last he does speak, we see at work a high intelligence, a fine education and a poetic power, all long restrained by the conditions of his self-exile in the Middle East. And his speeches are some of the most crabbed, contorted and agonized in English verse. Soon after his unburdening, he has left them, and Melville describes his sorrow on leaving his countrymen again after so long apart from them.

Attitudes to race had played a large part in Ungar's American life and, no doubt, in his self-imposed exile. The lack of racial discrimination in the Levant was perhaps one of its attractions for him. When he finds himself among his compatriots, some of whom later contrast his high moral tone with his service under a foreign flag, Ungar raises this issue early:

> *As cruel as a Turk:* Whence came
> That proverb old as the crusades?
> From Anglo-Saxons. What are they? . . .
> The Anglo-Saxons—lacking grace
> To win the love of any race:
> Hated by myriads dispossessed
> Of rights—the Indians East and West.
> These pirates of the sphere! Grave looters—
> Grave, canting, Mammonite freebooters,
> Who in the name of Christ and Trade
> (Oh, bucklered forehead of the brass!)
> Deflower the world's last sylvan glade! . . .
> Respond to this: Old ballads sing
> Fair Christian children crucified
> By impious Jews: you've heard the thing:
> Yes, fable; but there's truth hard by:
> How many Hughs of Lincoln, say,
> Does Mammon in his mills, today,
> Crook, if he do not crucify?[1]

Here we have two stereotypes in play, the cruelty of the Turks and the blood-guilt of the Jews. Both stereotypes appear in the European

---

1. Herman Melville, *The Oxford Book of American Verse*, 1971, Oxford, p. 400. I have adopted the editor's omissions.

middle ages, the Turk from the time of the Crusades and the Jew, say, in the Prioress' Tale of Chaucer's *Canterbury Tales*. The Jewish stereotype derives from the tale of an English boy who is murdered and defiled for singing of Christ in the ghetto. This tale is recognized by the pilgrims as a slander, but Ungar goes on to stress that such lads have been crippled in large numbers in the industrial factories of England and America. Ungar's vision of the Anglo-Saxons as pirates chimes with Emerson's description of them as thieves and pirates of the universe, and we hear echoes of Coleridge's denunciation in *Fears in Solitude*. Still, Ungar is not without his own racial prejudices, as we shall see.

> Grave looters,
> Grave, canting, Mammonite free booters…

These people appeal to Christ and trade in the same breath. They are the Puritans and Protestants of England and America who managed to believe that their wealth, however acquired, was a sign of God's grace. The bucklered forehead of the brass is a symbol of their mental invulnerability, the impossibility of anyone finding a way to their minds and hearts. First they enslaved the East and West Indies, then they ransacked the globe, and finally they are the new iron-masters in the industrial mills. The ironmasters certainly destroyed sylvan glades, but Ungar's speaking here of the last glade resonates with the hunting out of the American Indians from their ancestral lands.

But these Christian masters of the plantations and factories are much less dreadful in Ungar's eyes than are their successors:

> Against pretences void or weak
> The impieties of "Progress" speak.
> What say *these*, in effect to God?
> "How profits it? And who art Thou
> That we should serve Thee? Of Thy ways
> No knowledge we desire; *new* ways
> We have found out, and better. Go—
> Depart from us; we do erase
> Thy sinecure: behold, the sun
> Stands still no more in Ajalon:

Depart from us!"—And if He do?
(And that He may, the Scripture says)
Is aught betwixt ye and the hells?[2]

Here Ungar bodily picks up the European and American enlight-enment of the 18th and 19th centuries and puts it down in the middle of the Holy Land some three millennia earlier. Voltaire confronts Jehovah at Sinai. Even now, the careful staging and the power of the blasphemy give a thrill, comparable, say, to Blake's *Proverbs of Hell*. The blasphemer faces down Jehovah in His own sacred stronghold and dismisses Him contemptuously as *passé*. His divine office has become a sinecure since he has ceased to perform His miracles in this place for His chosen people. The word 'erase' recalls Voltaire's *'ecrasez l'infame'* and also the ancient Egyptian practice of removing the inscribed cartouches of earlier rulers when they fell into disfa-vor. The erasure of God's sinecure here is a trifling matter, a tiny act and look! God is no more. The address to this non-existent God exactly parodies the high-flown language of the Old Testament as the blasphemer demeans and rejects its principle. These are uncom-fortable lines, a long way on from the impious and unreligious inva-sion of Emerson's hills.

They are also beautiful lines, Melville at his Elizabethan best. The rising inflections of the mockery work with the rhythms of the tet-rameter. We cannot but hear the scorn, and hearing it, we become complicit in the blasphemy. We have seen many accounts of the subtle difference between the intellectual act and other forms of knowing. But it is hard to think of one which presents the difference more starkly. And Melville's dramatization of the philosophical point leaves open a question, which Blake has already raised. Is the new science primarily positive, a means to humanity's great mate-rial benefit? Or is it negative, a way of discounting the spiritual and religious past? In Melville's presentation, the blasphemy is much more engaged in abusing the notion of God than in promoting a new order.

Ungar's speech on the impieties of progress is early in his unbur-

2. Op. cit., pp. 401–402.

dening, and it must have compounded the sense of mystery and self-estrangement around him. His powerful blasphemy in this place must have disconcerted these tourists between worlds, and perhaps with his mention of Ajalon he gestured towards it. For Ungar belongs in ways that they do not. And yet Ungar has been talking to Americans in his heart ever since he left America, and now the moment has come at last and he is actually with some Americans. And so his rhetorical strategies, his paradoxes and questions are unusually developed and refined. But his is a dark power, with far more of the darkness of that place than the pilgrims have so far encountered.

In the last lines quoted above, Ungar begins to sound like an Old Testament prophet newly returned from communing with God in the wilderness, and set now to berate the Children of Israel for their disobedience. But Ungar claims no such authority for his predictions:

> The human nature, the divine—
> Have both been proved by many a sign.
> 'Tis no astrologer and star.
> The world has now so old become,
> Historic memory goes so far
> Backward through long defiles of doom;
> Whoso consults it honestly,
> That mind grows prescient in degree;
> For man, like God, abides the same
> Always, through all variety
> Of woven garments to the frame.[3]

Our historic memory is now so vast that it is a barrier to the student, since there is so much to master. But not for Ungar. For him its range and depth provide the materials he needs to determine the course of events in the future. And we have already some evidence of his facility in this regard, with the references to the murdered Hugh of Lincoln and Gideon's experience at Ajalon in the Book of Joshua.

---

3. Op. cit., pp. 402–403.

Hypothesise:
If be a people which began
Without impediment, or let
From any ruling which foreran;
Even striving all things to forget
But this—the excellence of man
Left to himself, his natural bent,
His own devices and intent;
And if, in satire of the heaven,
A world, a new world have been given
For stage whereon to deploy the event;
If such a people be—well, well,
One hears the kettledrums of hell!
Exemplary act awaits its place
In drama of the human race.[4]

The first word here is crucial. What is Ungar describing? A Rousseauian paradise? The Garden of Eden? The founding fathers of America? If we could achieve for a moment Rousseau's ideal, how long would it last? May we not cite the South Sea Islanders as a settled human order untainted by the vices of our civilization? But then we remember Melville's own experience with these cannibals? Is Ungar describing what would happen if Rousseau's dream were realized anew? Or is this simply Edenic, a restatement of the necessary human propensity to fall? But then why a 'people' and where is God and his evening walks? And the same objection applies if we take Ungar to be speaking of the Pilgrim Fathers. Where is God? Think of Ungar's own Maryland. Or are we to take it that 'any ruling' here refers only to the interpretation of scripture and not to scripture itself or the Decalogue? This may fit Puritan American generally. Of course we have here all these possibilities. Ungar is finding ways to traverse several ranges of thought simultaneously.

But if we put Ungar's hypothetical people together with his account of the blasphemer who beards Jehovah, we see why his America here forgets the religious refugees of its origins. For this is the vision of the secular progressives who imagine an America free

4. Op. cit., p. 402.

66

of religion. And it is these people and this vision that Ungar supposes so prone to a catastrophic fall. And, of course, they do more closely approximate to the condition of Adam and Eve in the garden just before the Fall. For they too seem to have forgotten about God who was so close to them. If, as Ungar does, we suppose that the progressives were calling the tune in late 19th-century America, then his forcing of the model of the Fall on his country's future is apt. But, of course, it was entirely contrary to his companions' vision of that land of hope.

One of the pilgrims rises to Ungar's provocation and denies that America is doomed. Little is certain in history, he says, and America is protected from internal division by its immense wealth. There is no occasion there for the struggles between rich and poor which are destroying Europe. Ungar reads this interjection as a counter-provocation and is sensitive to the possibility that he is being guyed:

> 'True heart do ye bear
> In this discussion? or but trim
> To draw my monomania out,
> For monomania, past doubt
> Some of ye deem it. Yet I'll on.
> Yours seems a reasonable tone;
> But in the New World things make haste:
> Not only men, the *state* lives fast—
> Fast breeds the pregnant eggs and shells,
> The slumberous combustibles
> Sure to explode. 'Twill come, 'twill come!
> One demagogue can trouble much:
> How of a hundred thousand such?
> And universal suffrage lent
> To back them with brute element
> Overwhelming? What shall bind these seas
> Of rival sharp communities
> Unchristianised? Yea, but 'twill come!'
>   'What come?'
>   'Your Thirty Years (of) War.'
>   'Should fortune's favourable star
> Avert it?'
>   'Fortune? Nay, 'tis doom.'

'Then what comes after? spasms but tend
Ever, at last to quiet.'
                'Know,
Whatever happen in the end,
Be sure 'twill yield to one and all
New confirmation of the fall
Of Adam. Sequel may ensue,
Indeed, whose germs one now may view:
Myriads playing pygmy parts—
Debased into equality:
In glut of all material arts
A civic barbarism may be:
Man disennobled—brutalised
By popular science—atheised
Into a smatterer—'
                'Oh, oh!'
    'Yet knowing all self need to know
In self's base little fallacy;
Dead level or rank commonplace:
An Anglo-Saxon China, see,
May on your vast plains shame the race
In the Dark Ages of Democracy.'[5]

There is no great difficulty with the first part of Ungar's speech here except for its anti-democratic extremism. With Ungar we return to that illiberal strand of Romanticism which made its German exponents unpopular, earlier in the century. Three problems converge according to Ungar: rapid production in the armaments industry; universal suffrage and mass demagoguery; the decline of Christianity in, presumably black, white, and Hispanic communities. These three acting together will produce thirty years of civil war. It is hard to say when Ungar thinks this war will begin. On the one hand, the production of armaments is very rapid. On the other hand, the loss of a common Christian belief or beliefs must have seemed at some distance in time from the 1870s.

Have we here an early intimation of what Eisenhower called the military-industrial complex? It is the *State* which lives fast here.

5. Ibid., pp. 403–405.

Ungar supposes that since these weapons have been made they are sure to be used. But in this he may be naïve since they are still profitable, used or not. But if he fears this arms race of the government, he viscerally loathes democracy and the egalitarian ideal. And it is quite unclear why he should feel this, given his anti-slavery views and mixed ancestry. Indeed, the arms race may itself be an image of the growth of democracy. It is neither Christian nor Catholic to hate democracy in principle. It is certainly not Biblical, where the use of the lot is egalitarian if also theocratic. Ungar has dismissed Plato earlier in a line but there are echoes here of the *Gorgias* and the political taxonomy in the *Republic*. The speeding up connects with mass demagoguery and gives a sense of ferment which will boil apart the bonds holding America together. We think of the Kali Yuga whose duration is but a quarter of the Golden Age, and whose speed is correspondingly much faster.

Ungar was wrong to anticipate thirty years of civil war in America. But his other predictions, given his point of view, were more successful. The pygmy parts are the factory jobs which will displace the older forms of work. We are taught to think of the machine age as a liberation from tedious and strenuous manual work, but it is as reasonable to claim that those mechanical contrivances typically removed the higher mental functions of design and adaptation from human work, and so reduced everyone to tedium and strain. About the civic barbarism Ungar expresses an uncharacteristic uncertainty, though he seems clear enough on the glut of industrial overproduction. For my part, this is one of Ungar's best hits. The automobile streetscape reminds me of the exile's return in Seferis' poem—to 'a thousand sickle-bearing chariots.'

The next ten words from 'Man' to 'smatterer' are a remarkable instance of verbal compression. They would do very well as a description of this entire essay. They certainly deserve the expostulatory interjection over which Ungar rides without drawing breath. And this though he has just coined a neologism with 'atheised' and linked it to the very rare word 'smatterer.' Ungar is concerned with an aspect of the scientific revolution to which we have not attended much, its popularization. We have considered Blake's Newtonian universities and Emerson's young botanists, but Melville now calls into question the residues of the new science in the common understanding. A smattering of physics or biology provides the inexpert with just what they need to know and no more: they are purely material phenomena and produced accidentally, so they must just make the best of their meaningless lives. For Ungar that sense of the self is a complete misapprehension, and an ugly one. That this is how most people will come to think is for Ungar the highest of the prices we pay for this progress. He thinks the new sciences much more destructive of the common understanding than Wordsworth did in his *Preface*. For Wordsworth or in Wordsworth's time, the Enlightenment seemed to have made no real impression on the popular understanding at all.

At the end of his speech Ungar returns to his attack on equality, and imagines America, to its shame, as an Anglo-Saxon China. Is this racist? As Chinese faces are less distinguishable from each other to the eye which is unused to them, so they may stand here for the undifferentiated masses into which the American people will sink. These were the last years of the Manchu Dynasty in China after some centuries. From Manchuria in the north, their status as Chinese was as questionable as whether Macedonians were Greeks. The Manchus tended to maintain racial purity, and this at least freed the Chinese from providing imperial harems. But the effect was to render all Chinese absolutely equal to each other in one respect—they were not Manchu but subordinate in their own country.

Like Ungar and the illiberal German Romantics, Yeats too held to a vision of hierarchical society. His hard-riding country gentlemen he contrasted with the base-born products of base beds. Strange to think of the links between the ex-Confederate mercenary with his dreams of old-world America, and Yeats at Coole Park. In *The Phases of the Moon* Yeats sees history as cycles of the moon from dark to dark again. At the end of the cycle, as the moon wanes from its last quarter, Yeats imagines a humanity which has almost entirely lost all the distinctions between individuals. He compares this mass to dough which Dame Nature is kneading up, ready to bake during the dark of the moon, for there is no human life at the dark. And then she wheels round the first thin crescent at the New Moon. This dough is Yeats' version of Ungar's America to come. And there is a sure sign that Ungar's fears of this egalitarianism were prescient. For it is now quite difficult to understand how Ungar could have feared such an ideal, and it is embarrassing and slightly mad that he should express such strictures.

But Ungar's American companions were not embarrassed by this final speech of his. A friendly peace settles on them as they contemplate together their distant country:

> America!
>> In stilled estate,
> On him, half-brother and co-mate—
> In silence, and with vision dim
> Rolfe, Vine, and Clarel gazed on him,
> They gazed, nor one of them found heart
> To upbraid the crotchet of his smart…
> Nor dull they were in honest tone
> To some misgivings of their own:
> They felt how far beyond the scope
> Of elder Europe's saddest thought
> Might be the New World's sudden brought
> In youth to share old age's pains—
> To feel the arrest of hope's advance,
> And squandered last inheritance;
> And cry—'To Terminus build fanes!
> Columbus ended earth's romance'
> No New World to mankind remains!

The Americans in the group are bound together by at least one common conception: the difference between America's destiny and the history of Europe. But their shared feeling is that America's destiny lies beyond Europe's saddest thought, not beyond Europe's happiest. For America must experience in its youth, the old age of the civilization from which many of its founding peoples came. They cannot begin again because they came inescapably from that earlier era. That era had been hopeful from the early Greeks onwards but now it was closing, and America was bound up in that closing. Indeed, America was a profound symbol of the closing. With its discovery, the geographical open-endedness of our globe, its pure possibility, was over.

6

Edwin Arlington Robinson

I N ROBINSON's *The Man against the Sky* the Romantic intellect confronts the sciences of economics and evolutionary biology. The book of poems of which this is the title poem was published in 1916 and won fame for its author. But this is a dark and difficult poem and its warm reception by the reading public showed discrimination. Despair is the subject of the poem though it is not shared by the poet.

The form of the poem is simple. Looking westward at a bare hill against a flaming sunset, the poet sees a man walk across the brow of the hill and disappear over the other side. The poet takes this man as a representative of his time and speculates on his destiny. The flaming sky is the backdrop to the poem until it ends in a darkness deeper than night. Here is Robinson's version of Emerson's young scholars and Wordsworth's miracle of scientific lore:

> Or maybe there, like many another one
> Who might have stood aloft and looked ahead,
> Black-drawn against wild red,
> He may have built, unawed by fiery gules
> That in him no commotion stirred,
> A living reason out of molecules
> Why molecules occurred,
> And one for smiling when he might have sighed
> Had he seen far enough,
> And in the same inevitable stuff
> Discovered an odd reason too for pride
> In being what he must have been by laws
> Infrangible and for no kind of cause.
> Deterred by no confusion or surprise

> He may have seen with his mechanic eyes
> A world without a meaning, and had room,
> Alone amid magnificence and doom,
> To build himself an airy monument
> That should, or fail him in his vague intent,
> Outlast an accidental universe—
> To call it nothing worse—[1]

This is an affectionate sketch of the scientistic mentality which, as the first line says, is quite common. Such people may not be moved by a sunset but they have a distinctive sense of humor. Robinson's account is even more inward than Wordsworth's as an understanding of this mindset. Those mechanic eyes smile at the purely atomistic universe, and this recalls Democritus, the laughing philosopher and first great atomist. That smile is a wry dismissal, but Robinson gives these people credit for changing their attitude if they were to see the sad outcome of their thinking. There is humor, too, in the tension between the infrangible laws and the no kind of cause. For these people primary causes do not exist, and so secondary mechanical causes have become absolute as well as invariable. The laws of physics cannot be broken but they are entirely accidental and meaningless. To acknowledge this and carry on takes courage. As for the airy monument, this sounds like the materialist epistemology of a Bertrand Russell, say, or a David Armstrong, heroes who have at least finally nailed the nonsense of it all.

We all know such people and they do indeed take pride in being more realistic than the rest of us. They are charming and self-deprecating and clever. And they are ambitious intellectually, though that is not the word. They are rather different from those early Atomists in the garden with Epicurus. Those people were as austere as any in antiquity, refugees from a world in confusion and seeking only a personal serenity. But our present mechanics are our rulers. Their resistance to anything beyond the laboratory or observatory is now dominant. They have made up their minds, whether or not they insult the rest of us, and they see no need to explain:

---

1. Edwin Arlington Robinson, *The Oxford Book of American Verse*, 1971, Oxford, pp. 500–501.

> Or tell us why one man in five
> Should have a care to stay alive
> While in his heart he feels no violence
> Laid on his humor and intelligence
> When infant Science makes a pleasant face
> And waves again that hollow toy, the Race;[2]

Four out of five men can see no reason to exist on the scientific world view. This pointlessness is the subject of the poem's second half. The human race is pointless, to assist its progress is pointless. We have no justification for bringing children into the world:

> What then were this great love of ours to say
> For launching other lives to voyage again
> A little farther into time and pain,
> A little faster in a futile chase
> For a kingdom and a power and a Race
> That would have still in sight
> A manifest end of ashes and eternal night?[3]

But surely, it may be said, those four out of five men do have a care to stay alive, however insulted they may feel themselves by atomism. Our great love may have no reason to give for producing children, but we still have children. Any demoralization, if it has occurred at all, has been very limited even up to the present time. And who is doing the demoralizing here? The mechanists are not insisting that we have no reason to live nor to have children. It is Robinson. We have here to deal with narrow moral distinctions between warning people of danger and being a danger oneself. We must beware of the man who shouts 'fire' in a crowded theatre without cause.

But Robinson is merely pointing out that the scientific world-view gives us no reason for staying here or having children. The reason which people once had no longer works. For we have lost sight of the intellectual principle, reunion with which by saint or sage bridges part of the distance between ourselves and the blissful omniscience of the Divine.

2. Op. cit., pp. 503–504.
3. Ibid., p. 50.

Where was he going, this man against the sky?
You know not, nor do I.
But this we know, if we know anything:
That we may laugh and fight and sing
And of our transience here make offering
To an orient Word that will not be erased,
Or, save in incommunicable gleams
Too permanent for dreams,
Be found or known.
No tonic and ambitious irritant
Of increase or of want
Has made an otherwise insensate waste
Of ages overthrown
A ruthless, veiled, implacable foretaste
Of other ages that are still to be
Depleted and rewarded variously
Because a few, by fate's economy,
Shall seem to move the world the way it goes;[4]

The orient Word which cannot be erased echoes Ungar's account of the erasing of God's sinecure, which may itself have echoed Voltaire. But this orient Word of Robinson is not easy to place or determine. We note that not only laughing and singing but fighting also may be offered to it. There are at least two major traditions which use the word or *logos* as principle: the maxims of Heraclitus who lived in Asia Minor about 500 BC and the doctrine of Christ as the *logos* in the first verses of St. John's gospel. To which, if either, is Robinson referring? The Heraclitean *logos* is not instantiated in the historical figure of a Saviour. It has to do rather with the necessity at the core of all oppositions in the world, and with the unity at the core of opposition itself:

> War is both king of all and father of all, and it has revealed some as gods, others as men; some it has made slaves, others free.[5]

It is not the animal spirits of investors, nor economic scarcity which drives history, but the orient Word. This it is which has made the

4. Op. cit., p. 503.
5. Heraclitus, Fragment 53.

ages up to now a grim foretaste of the ages to come. These ages, too, will have their various economic successes and failures. And it will seem to those people as it seems to us, that what happens to them is determined by their leaders. But that is wrong, it is the orient Word which has brought it all about. This vision is prophetic over a much larger time-scale than the Capitalist or Marxian, and it is quite unredeemed. There has never been nor can there ever be a solution to the problems of the human condition on earth. Is this Hera-clitean or Christian or neither? Robinson says here that our leaders only seem to move the world, but in fact they do so by fate's econ-omy. Fate is Greco-Roman rather than Judaeo-Christian. When we consider the lives and struggles of our entire species around the globe till now and project that forward again into the future, we may feel that Fate rather than the incarnate Word is the agency. To know some of the history of the race and to project it forward is exactly to live with an awareness of Fate. That is our condition. In this perspective of the ages, economic motives and human ambi-tions are mere irritants. The theories of economic historians are absurdly underpowered as an explanation of Fate's economy.

The orient Word and Fate sacralize human history and the human future without blinking at them. On the contrary, these lines describing the ages are exceptionally hopeless, and the divine powers which preside over the ages are terrible and forbidding. But they are worshipful, and they are adequate to their task. But when Robinson is asked to understand human history in economic terms, he cannot limit his scope as required. He finds economic explana-tions trifling, even grotesque, as a way of giving point to the human experience as a whole. His orient Word and his Fate name the dread which his lines inspire on the insensate waste of past and to come. These names too are inadequate, but at least they are terrible, not footling. Robinson's target here is not the science of economics as such, but theories like dialectical materialism which suppose eco-nomic explanations ultimate.

What is the 'otherwise insensate waste of ages overthrown'? All that is left of those ages, their only flicker of life, is what they show us now of future ages, which will implacably be like them. That is the lesson of those earlier ages which brings them to life. We see their likeness to ourselves and we project that continuity into the future. Ungar spoke of the vastness of history now, and how a deep historical learning enabled a kind of prescience. So there is one thing which is saved from all those earlier empires and civilizations, the way they ground us in the limitations of time as soon as we know of them. And such knowledge is essential to us as human, and the orient Word has prepared it for us. To accommodate that knowledge also demands courage and pride. But the orient Word is at least a word, though like the tetragrammaton it is beyond the human grasp.

Robinson continues:

> No planetary trap where souls are wrought
> For nothing but the sake of being caught
> And sent again to nothing will attune
> Itself to any key of any reason
> Why man should hunger through another season
> To find out why 'twere better late than soon
> To go away and let the sun and moon
> And all the silly stars illuminate
> A place for creeping things,
> And those that root and trumpet and have wings,
> And herd and ruminate,
> Or dive and flash and poise in rivers and seas,
> Or by their loyal tails in lofty trees
> Hang screeching lewd victorious derision
> Of man's immortal vision.[6]

Why do people struggle to go on living and have children? Heraclitus describes us:

> Being born, they are willing to live and meet their deaths, or rather rest, and they leave children after them to meet their deaths.[7]

This is a chilling aphorism since it gives people no reason for what they do, though there is some comfort in their thinking of death as rest. But according to Robinson, evolutionary theory leaves us even more bereft of reasons. Before, Man longed to know whether it was

6. Robinson, op. cit., p. 504.
7. Heraclitus, Fragment 20.

78

better to die young or old, and so struggled on with life in the hope of discovering the answer. But with evolutionary theory, the answer is in. The evolutionist knows that there is no point to human existence, no way of its making sense in human terms. So there is no point in living any longer, if we were living longer only in the hope of finding out. We have now found out, and it is not better to die old than young.

So Man should go away and let the sun, moon, and stars illuminate a non-human world. We should forego our ecological niche as a species and disappear since there is nothing to confer on us the slightest significance. Now it is one thing to have no care to stay alive, but to go away here seems to imply more than merely letting oneself die when ones time comes. To go away suggest a more positive and determined action, even suicide, even mass suicide since the whole race is to be taken out of the equation. This terrible suggestion is only a suggestion in the other sense, a hint or overtone, but it is there. And the futility and disgust with human life on these terms is felt in the blasphemy of the phrase 'silly stars.'

But when the stars are silly and the earth is a place for creeping things only, it has its own integrity and vibrant energy. The zoosphere here is described almost entirely by verbs until the end. And it seems to be especially lovely without us. It is impossible not to enjoy the lewdness of the monkeys as they celebrate their victory over our exploded spiritual delusions and our mass departure. For my part, I have always suspected that the animals worship too since, as Plato says, humans are merely the most reverent of creatures. We are the high priests of a very large clergy, so that the loss of the human race would irreparably damage the practice of many liturgies.

Robinson has an odd way with arguments. Economic scientism claims to plumb the well-springs of human history, so he confronts this science with the abyss of the ages. He evokes those ages in the grimmest terms and denies that any economic agency could move such a juggernaut. He claims that leaders merely seem to lead, and fate is over all. This is an argument from the incomparability of magnitudes: here are economic explanations of history; there is history; the two are on entirely different scales. With Darwinism, he entertains the thesis and deduces that it gives no reason to live. He then imagines an earth without human beings and very active it is. With the greatest good nature he allows monkeys the last laugh, who have at least loyal tails to hang on by. For they are surely wiser in their kind, in Darwin's view, than the creationists are in theirs.

Here is the last section of the poem:

> Shall we, because Eternity records
> Too vast an answer for the time-born words
> We spell, whereof so many are dead that once
> In our capricious lexicons
> Were so alive and final, hear no more
> The Word itself, the living word
> That none alive has ever heard
> Or ever spelt,
> And few have ever felt
> Without the fears and old surrenderings
> And terrors that began
> When Death let fall a feather from his wings
> And humbled the first man?
> Because the weight of our humility
> Wherefrom we gain
> A little wisdom and much pain,
> Falls here too sore and there too tedious,
> Are we in anguish or complacency,
> Not looking far enough ahead
> To see by what mad couriers we are led
> Along the roads of the ridiculous,
> To pity ourselves and laugh at faith
> And while we curse life bear it?
> And if we see the soul's dead end in death,
> Are we to fear it?
> What folly is here that has not yet a name
> Unless we say outright that we are liars?
> What have we seen beyond our sunset fires
> That lights again the way by which we came?
> Why pay we such a price, and one we give
> So clamoringly, for each racked empty day
> That leads one more last human hope away,
> As quiet fiends would lead past our crazed eyes

Our children to an unseen sacrifice?
If after all that we have lived and thought
All comes to Nought,—
If there be nothing after Now,
And we be nothing anyhow,
And we know that,—why live?
'Twere sure but weaklings' vain distress
To suffer dungeons where so many doors
Will open on the cold eternal shores
That look sheer down
To the dark tideless floods of Nothingness
Where all who know may drown.[8]

This passage begins with a single, long question. At first reading the question may appear to be: Shall we hear the living word which none alive has ever heard? And the answer to this question is clearly no. But Robinson does not say nor imply that none alive has ever heard this Word. He says that none alive has ever heard it without being terrified. Nor has anyone ever spelt it without being terrified. Of all those who have merely felt it, a few may have done so without being terrified. Given the poem up to now, we expect the claim that Robinson and his generation are precluded by their new sciences from hearing the living Word. But the perspective implicit in this question is much broader than his time. It is fundamental to the human state that an encounter with God terrifies us, and no one while alive undergoes any close encounter without fear. So the 'none alive' here does not mean 'no one now living' but 'no one while alive.'

But Robinson still asks whether he and his readers can hear that Word. For they have heard of such a multitude of Gods who have come and gone that they can no longer take any of them seriously. So perhaps our time does have a special problem which other ages did not fully share. On the other hand, the insight that no name suffices for this purpose is made clear by the first characters of the *Tao To Ching*, the maxims of Heraclitus and the *Mystical Theology* of Pseudo-Dionysius. It is hard to see how this graveyard of names will hinder our perception of eternity.

8. Robinson, op. cit., pp. 504–505.

So Robinson's question has become: Shall we, despite the loss of so many holy names, still hear or spell the Word and be terrified? Or, shall we at least feel the Word with or without being terrified? And the answer to these questions is surely yes. On this reading, Robinson's question might at a stretch be addressed to a religious congregation, to elicit joyful affirmations of their continued competence.

With his question, Robinson re-establishes the intellectual principle as the goal of the human search. He has shown the incapacity of atomism, economic scientism and evolutionism to provide any reason why human beings should live and reproduce. He now restores the grand purpose of the human race in the universe as it was always known to be before the Enlightenment. But Robinson's view of the encounter between the human and the divine is that it is frightening in the way that death is frightening. This is very different from the *uniones mysticae* of Wordsworth, Coleridge, and Keats. For Robinson, the egotistical sublime seems quite dissolved in fear and trembling. The model is rather of Moses at Sinai, whose summit no one else could approach or they would surely suffer death. A parallel to this is Wordsworth's 'high instincts before which our mortal nature did tremble like a guilty thing surprised.' The Graeco-Roman tradition is much less concerned with fearing the divine than is the Judaeo-Christian, at least at the level of contemplation. But here even this terror is turned a little aside by the gentleness of that single feather's fall.

The long opening question and its implied answer are the best that can be said of Robinson and his readers in this finale. After this question, the remaining lines are a continuous lament over their supine acceptance of an absurd world-view. Their leaders are mad and the paths down which they take the people are ridiculous. But this absurdity modulates into the much more sinister picture of the pointless days as quiet fiends leading their children away to an unseen sacrifice. Here the children stand for all their spiritual hopes, their 'immortal vision.'

The very last lines of the poem are exceptionally challenging. For they seem to advocate suicide, though only under certain circumstances. But the advocacy of suicide is a counsel of despair, and despair is the sin against the Holy Ghost, and unforgivable in the Christian tradition. For Socrates, suicide was desertion from the posts to which Zeus had appointed us in our watch-towers. The conditions or circumstances in which Robinson advocates suicide are these: the candidate believes in the atomistic, scientistic universe and is thoroughly and vocally miserable. Robinson supposes that such people are weaklings for not killing themselves, and that their distress in life deserves no sympathy, since the complete solution, from their point of view, lies immediately to hand. But was the Count of Monte Cristo a coward for enduring the Chateau D'If, or those prisoners who sing of their liberation in *Fidelio*? But these prisoners could hope for a liberation all too imaginable. The atomist who knows can have no such hope. Robinson is very careful to stress here how these putative suicides know that there is nothing after death, and this is the governing idea again in the very last line.

So perhaps we may state the argument of these very last lines as follows: anyone who claims to know that there is nothing after death and that there are no first causes is quite defenceless against the demand that they suicide if they feel that life is not worth the candle. So either they never complain 'more clamoringly', or they drop their nihilistic certainties, or they kill themselves. It is only if they fail to do one or more of these three things, that we may account them cowards and weaklings and feel no sympathy for their distress. Again, it is only those who know who may drown in the last line. What they know is that the scientistic world view is correct and the only one. But nobody could ever know this, since it is not true. And therefore nobody may drown, and these lines do not advocate suicide.

But if Robinson is not homicidal here, he is incensed beyond anything we have seen since Blake's *Milton*. He is forcing the nihilistic mechanists and atomists just as hard as he can. His earlier account of the mechanist captured a certain wry humor in his subject, but his affectionate picture there does little to mitigate the contempt for science and the scientists throughout the latter part of the poem. It is infant science waving a hollow toy; crass chance; a futile chase; a violence done to the humor and intelligence of almost all of us; which cannot attune itself to any key of any reason why we should go on living. Science is a mad courier into the ridiculous, and Robinson does indeed wish it on into the nullity it proclaims.

✤

Blake wrote:

> He who replies to words of Doubt
> Doth put the Light of Knowledge out.

These poets have not the least interest in a debate about creationism or the reality of God or the existence of other minds. Like Wittgenstein, they think there is something mad about the thought that the liveliness of children is mere automatism. This is the nullity which Blake, Melville and Robinson can sense in the scientists. To these poets, scientists are the strangest creatures imaginable, completely contained in self's base little fallacy.

Since C.P. Snow we have been calling the literary and scientific elements in our universities and general life 'the two cultures.' This, too, is quite incorrect, since the new sciences are not concerned with the culture and development of humanity. They are concerned with a certain controlling of nature for the purposes of very few among us and to the advantage of none. The actual goal of humanity is the intellectual reunion of the all in One, which is pursued in many ways but always on the clear understanding that there neither is nor can be any higher goal than this. The Romantics reaffirmed this in the midst of the Enlightenment. They were a comfort to thinkers in their own times and have been ever since. And they will be an especial comfort in those times to come when the selfishness, violence and intellectual vacuity of the new sciences will become quite apparent. Then the Romantics will show us that what is being lost was not worth having. It was a mere discontinuity in the progress of humankind, a darkness lit by brilliant stars.

Conclusion

To Romanticize means to endow base matters with noble meaning, ordinary matters with a mysterious status, familiar matters
with the dignity of the unknown, finite matter with the appearance of infinity.

Novalis

> To see a World in a Grain of Sand
> And a heaven in a Wild Flower,
> Hold Infinity in the palm of your hand
> And Eternity in an hour.[1]

Wm Blake

We have noted how Blake and Novalis both used a mill
driven by a water-wheel to represent the mechanical
universe of Enlightenment cosmologies. But while Novalis and his friends called themselves Romantics and the term was
soon adopted by a school of French poets, the term 'Romantic' was
not applied to English authors such as Blake, Coleridge and Wordsworth, until the 1880s. This is still the case with the entry in the
Chambers Encyclopaedia of 1883.

ROMANTIC SCHOOL, the name first assumed in Germany
about the beginning of the present century, by a number of young
poets and critics, A.W. and Fr. Schlegel, Novalis, Ludwig Tieck,
Wackenroder, etc., who wished to indicate by the designation that
they sought the essence of art and poetry in the wonderful and
fantastic elements that pre-eminently characterised the Romance
literature of the middle ages. Their efforts were directed to the
overthrow of the artificial rhetoric and unimaginative pedantry of
the French school of poetry, even then influential, and to the res-
toration of a belief in the mystery and wonder that enveloped the
existence of man—a belief that had been rudely assailed and
mocked by the prevailing materialism in all departments of

---

1. Blake, *K.* 431, *Aug* 1–4.

thought. Thus, their purpose was twofold—it was in part aesthetic, and in part religious. As poetical reformers the Romantic school in Germany unquestionably exercised a most beneficial influence; but as religionists—though their aim was intrinsically high and noble—they more or less consciously subserved the designs of a reactionary government and so came to be hated and distrusted by the liberal politicians and thinkers of Germany.

Between twenty and thirty years later, a similar school arose in France, and had a long struggle for supremacy with the older Classic school. It was victorious, but not wise, and except in a few instances—such as Lamartine and Victor Hugo—it has rushed into excesses of caprice both literary and moral, which have stamped it with a revolutionary rather than a reformatory character.

The account here of German Romanticism applies at almost every point to Blake, Wordsworth and Coleridge. Here again is a literature devoted to wonder in the light of common day. Their rejection of artifice in English poetry is heard in Blake's casting off of paltry rhymes, and Wordsworth's purification of English verse in the *Preface to the Lyrical Ballads*. The *Chambers Encyclopaedia* is sympathetic to the German Romantics' love of wonder and to their response when confronted by the materialists' insensitivity and derision. Refreshingly for an encyclopaedia, it is much more supportive of Romantic wonder than of the Enlighteners and Encyclopaedists. We have seen this power of awe in the three English Romantics. Again, like the Germans, the English Romantics became a *de facto* priesthood for want of Church leadership in these new spiritual wars against scientism. The only point at which this encyclopaedia's account of the German Romantics does not apply to the English Romantics is their politics. All the English Romantics were revolutionary when young.

The German Romantics' resistance to scientific materialism is echoed in Yeats' description of the English Romantics:

The mischief began at the end of the 17th century when men became passive before a mechanised nature, which has lasted to our own day, with a brief intermission between Smart's *Song of*

David and the death of Byron, wherein imprisoned man beat upon the door.[2]

Let us attempt our own encyclopaedic definition:

ROMANTICISM, the name of a philosophical and artistic movement in Germany and England about 1800. Of the German Romantics, Novalis, the Schlegel brothers, Schiller and Schelling are the best known; of the English Romantics, Blake, Wordsworth and Coleridge. Wordsworth and Coleridge visited Germany, but the same spirit seems to have moved the English and German Romantics quite independently.

For the Romantics, poetry was still a major medium of philosophy and they continued to believe in ancient and medieval conceptions of human destiny. They believed that our purpose is to know God directly. For them the faculty of intellection and the Being which it contemplates were central. Alike, the German and English Romantics denied that this Being, the ultimate goal of science, could be approached through empirical methods. They supposed that the Enlightenment had erred when it deprecated and discounted Classical and Christian visions of human fulfilment. On these grounds they rejected much of Bacon, Descartes, Newton, Locke, Voltaire and Hume, and they hoped for the return of a natural philosophy in which Nature was animated, not mechanical.

Romanticism has been influential in Britain and America: Keats and Shelley, William Morris and Yeats, and, on this account, T. S. Eliot; Emerson and Poe, Thoreau, Melville and Robinson. These writers opposed the Enlightenment's conception of science and believed Plato, Aristotle, even Dante more scientific. Romanticism was and is the Counter-Enlightenment, and it was concerned from the beginning with scientific epistemology and ontology. Any Westerner who has maintained a religious belief despite the Enlightenment is a Romantic. Any believer, West or East, who has to deal with scientistic modernity, will find in the Romantic philosophers a rock and a refuge.

This account of Romanticism is a standard one, but no longer in fashion. More recently, University critics have emphasised the variety of uses to which the word 'Romantic' has been put. If we

2. W. B. Yeats, *Introduction to the Oxford Book of Modern Verse*, Oxford, 1935.

grant this usage, the older definition is unsatisfactory. Byron, for example, is hardly a Romantic on the standard account, yet in Continental Europe he was regarded as the exemplary English Romantic; again, nowhere else is T.S. Eliot a Romantic as he is here. On the other hand, the Romantic intellect is central to the Romantic program from the beginning of its history, and must be acknowledged. Furthermore, the Romantic intellect remains powerful to this day. Enlightenment conceptions of science have been no more alive in our laboratories, than their Romantic contradictions in all the arts. The conjunction of the Arts and Sciences in universities has yielded a critique of Romanticism which evades its challenge to the scientific materialism of our time.

To compare ancient and medieval philosophy with our own debates about science is to see that very little has changed. All the old schools of philosophy are still in play; the mould-breaking science of the Enlighteners has not removed one. As the Enlighteners had been the return of Democritus, Epicurus and Lucretius, the Romantics were the recrudescence of Platonic and medieval mysticism. In the great and permanent variety of philosophical views, not all are equally consistent in themselves, nor are they all equally profound accounts of the world. Their ineluctable plurality may have to do, rather, with a certain pattern of predispositions in almost every human collective. But all the views are almost always there simultaneously or over time. The only change is in their relative strength and exposure. Still more beset by doubters than the Classical and Christian theologians, the Romantics revealed in their writings a direct and lovely knowledge of the divine. They did so in terms scarcely bounded by any tradition and so approachable by all. Romanticism was and is a reaction to the Enlightenment, and it began in the same places a little later. The antidote grew up by the poison and is as universal.

MISCELLANY

Two Philosophy Tutorials

I.
On Evolution

TUTOR

Come in! Not too wet? Today I think we have 'Aristotle on Evolution'? And you have the passage from the *Physics* in the handout? Excellent! Well, fire away and we'll see what you make of it.

STUDENT

Er, I don't have a full essay written this time! I've made pages of notes but I can't seem to bring them together in a continuous piece.

TUTOR

...well, all right. Start off by reading the Aristotle from the beginning until I stop you. Then we'll talk about it. You've given me this note business before.

STUDENT

We must now consider why Nature is to be ranked among causes that are final, that is to say purposeful; and further we must consider what is meant by 'necessity' when we are speaking of Nature. For thinkers are for ever referring things to necessity as a cause, and explaining that, since hot and cold and so forth are what they are, this or that exists or comes into being 'of necessity'; for even if one or another of them alleges some other cause, such as 'Sympathy and Antipathy', he straight away drops it again, after a mere acknowledgment.

So here the question rises whether we have any reason to regard Nature as making for any goal at all, or as seeking any one thing as preferable to any other. Why not say, it is asked, that Nature acts as Zeus drops the rain, not to make the corn grow, but of necessity (for the rising vapor must needs be condensed into water by the cold, and must then descend, and incidentally, when this happens the corn grows), just as, when a man loses his corn on the thresh-

91

ing-floor, it did not rain on purpose to destroy the crop, but the result was merely incidental to the raining? So why should it not be the same with natural organs like the teeth? Why should it not be a coincidence that the front teeth come up with an edge, suited to dividing the food, and the back ones flat and good for grinding it, without there being any design in the matter? And so with all other organs that seem to embody a purpose. In cases where a coincidence brought about such a combination as might have been arranged on purpose, the creatures, it is urged, having been suitably formed by the operation of chance, survived; otherwise they perished, and still perish, as Empedocles says of his 'man-faced oxen.' Such and suchlike are the arguments which may be urged in raising this problem; but it is impossible that this should really be the way of it. For all these phenomena and all natural things are either constant or normal, and this is contrary to the very meaning of luck or chance. . . .[1]

TUTOR

Thank you. Any thoughts?

STUDENT

I think Aristotle goes wrong from the end of the first paragraph. He wants Nature to be purposeful and for him this means that what happens or exists is not the result of necessity. But modern science is not teleological. It is about discovering quantifiable laws which apply in Nature without exception in every case of a given kind. So modern science seems to me to be necessitarian in exactly the way that displeases Aristotle about some scientists of his time.

TUTOR

Be careful how you use that word 'necessitarian.' In theology it signifies a disbelief in human free will. I think what you are describing is now called 'methodological naturalism.' But all right, you think your non-teleological and necessitarian explanations more scientific than Aristotle's purposeful Nature. Can't we have both? For example Leibniz thought there were two worlds, one of things, the

---

1. Aristotle, *Physics II*, 8, tr: Wicksteed and Cornford, Loeb.

other of minds, and these two were perfectly coordinated. Everything happened according to natural law to the greater glory of God and the salvation of souls.

TUTOR

STUDENT

Well, if you're going to believe something like that, you'll be better off forgetting philosophy and just going to church! At least Aristotle isn't saying that!

TUTOR

Anyway, you haven't explained how your theory of necessity applies to the rest of what Aristotle says. You are sympathetic, I take it, to the theory of accidental organic development which Aristotle rejects.

STUDENT

Yes.

TUTOR

But surely this theory is hardly necessitarian. It supposes a chaotic proliferation of random forms, out of which accidentally some are capable of survival. Where's the necessity here?

STUDENT

If you grant a sufficiently large and varied pool of life-forms, generated and generating randomly, and situate this pool in a relentless environment, it will necessarily happen that some creatures will be equipped by accident to cope with that environment where most will perish. Through reproduction these viable forms will eventually and necessarily occupy all the available living space, ousting the less viable.

TUTOR

Hold on! I thought you began this with 'a sufficiently large and varied pool of life forms, generated and generating randomly'!

STUDENT

I did.

TUTOR

But suddenly they're not generating randomly but reproducing themselves. Those accidentally viable creatures magically acquired the power of speciation indefinitely, not only in their immediate issue but for as long as you like. There's nothing accidental or coincidental about this power, and that's why Aristotle says that purposeful organization in Nature is the only explanation.

STUDENT

If that pool of life-forms is truly random, then it will contain creatures which copulate and creatures which do not. Of those that copulate, some will procreate and most will not. Of those that procreate, some will reproduce themselves and most will not. Where a creature appears which is at once accidentally equipped by nature to survive and capable of reproducing itself, its offspring too will be equipped accidentally to survive, and perhaps reproduce themselves. When they can do so indefinitely they will, and eventually there will be many such creatures all equipped to survive and reproduce themselves, as a result of necessity working on randomness.

TUTOR

That would be a few steps too far for Aristotle. But even so, it would fall short of Darwin's theory of accidents and coincidences, wouldn't it?

STUDENT

I'm sorry?

TUTOR

Darwin supposes that these self-reproducing, coincidentally surviving creatures fortuitously produce small but crucial differences in the formations of their offspring. In some cases these mutations are still better suited to their environment and in these ways, slowly, even transpeciation can occur. So the primordial soup not only produces creatures accidentally fitted to survive and reproduce, but reproduce in such a way that they can modulate into new, more efficient species.

STUDENT

It is a very large pool.

TUTOR

And with each new level of improbability, you merely extend the zillions of possibilities by fiat, to render the new unlikelihood within the bounds of statistical possibility.

STUDENT

No. There is a single scientific explanation here of all the coincidences. This explanation may meet certain difficulties statistically, but then it all follows under a single law. The coincidence or statistical probability is what it is. The fact is that we are the only living creatures in this universe of whom we know, despite all experience and the most sophisticated research. That shows how rare is the particular conformation we find here on earth. If, as Aristotle says, Nature is purposive, why has she seeded space with all these worlds, on none of which, save ours, is there any evidence of life? It is to the norm of this lifeless extravagance that Aristotle should compare life on earth, and then it will seem as accidental and coincidental as the evolutionists suppose.

TUTOR

Yes, but for Aristotle the cosmos was a single living creature, as it was for Plato. Everything was animate. The stars and planets were intelligent and alive, and their movements in their precision demonstrated the perfected power of reason within their souls. So he would not have been much moved by your argument from the absence of extraterrestrial life.

STUDENT

That sounds a great deal more implausible than the theory of evolution which he rejects.

TUTOR

Perhaps, but there is an aspect to the evolutionists' implausibilities which we need to bring out. You say that you're a scientific necessitarian and you think that the natural world is to be explained by means of demonstrable and absolute laws, determined by the most accurate observation and experiment.

STUDENT

Yes.

TUTOR

So Aristotle's reliance on formal and final causes must be rejected as failing our scientific criteria, but the evolutionary theory which he rejects is acceptable because it relies on material and efficient causes only.

STUDENT

Yes.

TUTOR

So do you accept the evolutionary theory because it conforms to the scientific view and has no use for formal or final causes? Or do you accept the evolutionary theory on the basis of the evidence for it in its own right?

STUDENT

That's a very difficult question. Why do I have to choose? Why can't I accept Darwin's theory and its later modifications for both reasons?

TUTOR

Because of the improbabilities we have discussed. To take it as axiomatic that the universe operates in all cases in accordance with material and efficient causes only is to adopt the modern scientific world view. That may persuade one to believe in very improbable theories in order to preserve ones adoption of the world-view. Religions, of course, are notorious for the way they preserve their axioms in this way.

STUDENT

Are you saying that anyone who believes in evolution is as bad as a religious fanatic?

TUTOR

Not at all. Many natural scientists work on evolutionary principles in the lecture room and laboratory but worship a God who made Heaven and Earth. As I said before, the necessitarian axiom can be adopted to explain the world of nature and simultaneously there can be a belief in the providential government of our souls.

STUDENT

But what about evolutionists who don't believe in such a double system?

TUTOR

They must swallow the improbabilities of their single system without the help of condiments. Or we may say that though the evolutionary view conforms to scientific criteria, it is too improbable as stated and we must wait for a better scientific and necessitarian explanation of natural development.

Well, time is getting on and I think we've talked enough about Aristotle. How about the second part of your topic, 'the influence of evolutionary theory on popular thought now'?

STUDENT

For this bit I've got something continuous written down.

TUTOR

At last!

STUDENT

To understand the influence of evolutionary theory on popular thought, it will help if we look first at another more recent scientific theory: psychological eliminativism. This theory supposes that scientific developments in psychology, neurophysiology, and especially pharmacology, have rendered obsolete the folk-language once used to describe human thoughts and feelings. Once we said people were truculent or demanding, then we said they were aggressive, now we say they are on steroids. Once we said people were sad, then that they were depressed, now that they are on a downer. Even more profoundly, the very notion of the mind itself must be discarded in the light of what we know now. It too is part of that obsolete folk-language and has as little grip on the real nature of things as demonology or phlogiston theory. It is a ghost in the animal machine which must be exorcized now that our knowledge of that machine has developed.

Whether the eliminativists are right about the future of our thought and language, it is inescapable that evolutionary theory has already wrought an enormous transformation in both. Nature may be replete with the most varied and wonderful adaptations of means to ends and they may appear as masterpieces of intelligent design and purpose. But we need suppose no invisible creator to understand how it became so. For at least a thousand years the peoples of Europe had worshipped daily their father almighty, maker of heaven and earth. There have been many other influences at work but evolutionary theory has certainly played a part in the emptying of churches in many countries. It is true that in contrast to religious sentimentalism, the Darwinian world of struggle is indifferent. But I certainly do not think Darwinism was somehow meant to justify the state in the class struggles in the industrializing nations of the nineteenth century.

On the other hand it is impossible to ignore the startling parallels between evolutionary theory and the theory of Divine creation in Genesis. I dare say that there is in our epoch no other scriptural account of the making of the world as close to the evolutionary view as the first two chapters of the Old Testament. The orderly succession of stages and the late appearance of humans are two examples. Now it may be said that evolutionary theory has not had the effect on the synagogue or the mosque which it has had upon the Church. But these institutions, too, subscribe to the *Genesis* account. This, I think, is a matter of time. The *Genesis* view predisposed the European mind to evolutionary theory. What *Genesis* has helped to produce has seriously eclipsed it.

Evolutionary theory posed the second great intellectual challenge to the wisdom of the Church. The first was heliocentrism. But this time the source of the challenge was largely beyond the center's control. England had its own church which was weak, and Rome had no remit. The directness of the contradiction between evolutionary theory and Creationism gave a delightful frisson to many millions of believers. It was at once the most intense engagement in Church doctrine and the first full playing out of Enlightenment scientific rigor as an imaginative possibility. With the evolutionary debate, science came of age in northwestern Europe first, and then elsewhere. It became a popular institution.

The idea of Nature changed correspondingly though these changes are harder to pick. The thought that Nature was a mother became harder to sustain. If all the purpose in nature was the operation of necessity upon the random, then Nature might as well be the ancient Greek Goddess *Tyche,* or Chance. For the creatures in nature were not as they were by a superordinate agency which bound them to a particular dispensation. There was only their urge to survive and propagate themselves.

In this crucial respect the effect of evolutionary theory was unprecedented in the history of our epoch. In other revolutions, one dispensation replaced another. The Classical philosophers yielded to the Christian Fathers whose faithful sometimes yielded to Islam. But with Darwinism an old dispensation yielded for the first time to an ethical vacuum. Religion and ideology no longer played a part.

We must avoid overstatement here. The profound interrelationship between creation in *Genesis* and evolutionary theory made the struggle between them peculiarly intense in the popular imagination. *Genesis* had shaped that imagination for centuries. But this applies only to the Semitic traditions of Judaism, Christianity and Islam. Further East, God was still approached through the severities of meditation. In Hinduism, the creator God Brahma is but one among numerous others; in Buddhism, the consideration of how things originated in nature is otiose; in Taoism, one produced two, two three, and three the ten thousand creatures. None of these traditions is challenged by evolutionary theory.

But in the West Darwinism was and is very corrosive of established beliefs. Dante had said God made Nature and Nature made us, and we should follow them by becoming creators ourselves. Usurers did not create in the right way and so defied both God and Nature. Darwin helped mightily in the disestablishment of all this, though he did not begin it. The attempt to find an intrinsic justification for the social order dates at least from More's *Utopia.* But in Rousseau's Social Contract, Bentham's Utilitarianism, Mill's Libertarianism, and Marx's Communism, we see a new impetus in these efforts. With all this, Darwinism was entirely consonant, and helped in its turn to shape a movement which brings the absence of providential Nature sharply before us. Existence comes before essence, the slogan says, and is quite undetermined. But existence here was not Plato's Good or the One of Plotinus. It was simply each human's condition in a world which offered no directions. This reflected at depth the Darwinian theory and helped to stimulate a general anxiety in the Continental philosophers. In the Anglosphere the response was no less deep but much cooler. Thinkers there turned rather to the analysis of the earlier language and its deconstruction. One popular version of this is the belief that life has no meaning, which is often as mistaken as the belief that life has a meaning. The point is that meaning is a term which applies to propositions, say, or myths but not to human existence *in toto*. But that is point enough since it obviates the need to understand a human life in any context larger than its own lived existence. The meaning of life is the living.

In our progress towards a society founded on the principles of Enlightenment science, we are much further along the road than Darwin was and we should be grateful to his memory. We can dimly foresee a time when a humanity, a continent, a whole people will stand freely under the sky, with an appreciation of their origins unclouded by any fear or superstition of some higher mind which made them and will judge them. They will know that their 'selves' are merely 'the psychological idea', the Kantian precondition of subjective and objective experience. This 'self' is identical in every person, and as it is merely a precondition of our living experience, so it ends with that experience. We may ask of the stars 'Why me? Why am I here as a person?' And the answer is that necessity worked upon spontaneity and randomness and eventually produced people. During a certain period of development some people misconstrued their origins and even supposed that they existed beyond the human state. But, of course, they did not and such questions are absurd.

TUTOR

All right. At least that's nearly a full essay even if it's on the second part of the topic only. But even within those limits you seem to me to have made the classic mistake of examinees twice over.

STUDENT

I'm sorry?

TUTOR

The classic rule is ATQ: answer the question. The question concerned the influence of evolutionary theory on popular thought now. Now in the first place your paper was almost entirely concerned with writers and intellectual movements. On the one occasion when you do talk of much more intense class struggles in the industrializing nations of the nineteenth century, you dismiss any relation between this and evolutionary theory out of hand.

STUDENT

I thought it was far too vague. I do mention science as an institution in the popular imagination.

TUTOR

True, but even in your account of the writers and 'isms', you only get up to about 1935 and the Oxford positivists. Nothing on the last eighty years except the Eliminativists.

STUDENT

All right, I accept that but what about what I did do?

TUTOR

Well, we'll start there and then go on to what you didn't do but might have done. Your topic next fortnight is very similar, so you can quickly put right where you went wrong this time. The one big problem with your essay as it stands is your confusion about the status of Enlightenment science as an ideology.

STUDENT

I said it wasn't an ideology.

TUTOR

I know, but just before you read your essay you agreed that Enlightenment science depended on Necessity, on the necessititarian axiom that every event has material and efficient causes only, and that everything can be explained by these two kinds of causes alone.

STUDENT

I did.

TUTOR

But that fundamental axiom is an article of faith. It is itself beyond proof since it is the condition on which all that you account science is conducted. So important is it to maintain the axiom that even improbable theories like evolution are acceptable provided that they observe the principle and nothing more plausible is on offer. Isn't that ideological, indeed casuistical?

STUDENT

No. The scientific method is arguably open to all, at least in theory. Religious wisdom is the exclusive province of a few mystics.

TUTOR

I like your 'in theory.' How many amateurs own both a telescope and a microscope? And these people can't keep up even with the twentieth century. No, Science is as opaque as the Bible was to illiterates who didn't know its language.

STUDENT

You're joking!

TUTOR

And then consider the older universities. Those scholarly rooms were occupied once by clergymen, by and large, divines. And now they're occupied by Doctors of Science. Is the change effected by Enlightenment science really so great? I did like what you said about the consonances between *Genesis* and evolutionary theory. Isn't the same true of the university before and after the Enlightenment? Is not the scientific establishment with its synods, concilia and curiae just the old authoritarian, ideological order rebadged to keep it alive for another spin? Look at the shape, not the dazzle.

STUDENT

I still think there's a huge difference between the...

TUTOR

And so, no doubt, do the scientists themselves, but until you can say what that difference is, you had better not try to argue it. Still you'll have plenty of opportunities to make that case again. Let's go back to what you didn't do this time but might do next time.

STUDENT

OK.

TUTOR

You have no time for the view that the violence of the class-struggles in the nineteenth century was in some way represented in Darwin's vision of the universal struggle for survival in the natural world. Well, how about this? Let us suppose that in a middle-sized island, within a few decades of each other, two massive changes occurred to alter fundamentally the accepted wisdom of ages. First, the industrial revolution in the late eighteenth century began to displace and dispossess craftworkers in more and more crafts. For thousands of years, craftworkers, slave or free, separately and in factories, had been fundamental units of economic production. This began to unravel. A few decades later the notion that the cosmos was the work of an intelligent designer, Yahweh, Elohim, the Demiurge of Plato, was also undone. Jehovah and Plato's Craftsman were as irrelevant to the actual order of nature as the craftworker had become to the new economy. Now I agree that the relationship between these two changes is vague and hard to pin down. But surely it is there somehow?

STUDENT

I can see that there is a relation but I've no idea how to get at it.

TUTOR

That's why you're paying us the big money, to teach you. But let's go now to the other omission from your essay, the last eighty years. Tell me, is it true that we now see unemployment and underemployment in Europe on a large scale?

STUDENT

Yes.

TUTOR

But if craftwork is not Dante's imitation of God and Nature, nor any other form of work, does it matter that many are not working who could?

STUDENT

I'm not sure.

TUTOR

May it not be that the technological quantum leap by which we now provide for ourselves is the next stage in the evolutionary march? That we are, as you said, at last grown up, and we have at our adult fingertips powers undreamt in earlier times? And for this transformation the peoples of the developed nations have long been prepared by Science-fiction in all the forms of our modern media?

STUDENT

That has been contemporary ever since Verne and Wells.

TUTOR

Or maybe it goes another way? That we're seeing merely the next stage of the many stages by which financiers, inventors and mechanics have successively acquired the work and wages of almost every other occupation? That a population long enough subjected to this will eventually give up, since the dole and the playing of video games are not enough reasons to reproduce ourself and raise a family. It is not like handing on your workshop to your son. And so they dwindle quietly and in a few generations cease, teetering for a while at the cliff edge. In their own terms they painted the globe red, but they will not be defeated by ICBMs nor huge land wars. It is just demographics. And some historian later might wryly remark that the evolutionary theory seems to have had a distinctly anti-evolutionary effect on the first nation to adopt it.

STUDENT

Phew!

TUTOR

Well, you see it is full of fascinating possibilities. And I want to hear some of them in your next essay which will, no doubt, cover all the parts of the topic. No more notes. I've told you before that higher degrees in Philosophy by course work in this University are not easily come by.

STUDENT

OK, OK, I know that the exams are coming on and I must answer all parts of the question better. But which of those two futures you just described do you think more likely?

TUTOR

I don't think it matters. What matters is that we don't know. The possibility of some kind of mass human transformation into work-lessness has got mixed up in our minds with evolutionary development. By this point, I think, the dispossessed farming, artisanal and small retailing classes should have reasserted their right to work and set limits to industrialization and the big end of town. But the possibility of a society in which work is transcended, has confused these classes in both Capitalist and Communist states. The new media compound the effect. They supplant our perception of what is actually going on around us, not only by what they broadcast but by the miracle of their doing so. Like heroin they so occupy our minds with imaginings, we forget the discomfort we're actually in. But enough, it is well over our usual time.

II.
On Automation

TUTOR

Come in! How are you? Well, this fortnight it's 'Plato and Automation.' How did you find those passages from the *Republic?*

STUDENT

Very lovable. Much warmer than Aristotle.

TUTOR

Really. 'Lovable'? That's an odd word for Plato. I hope you explain it in your essay.

STUDENT

I try a bit later on. I start with a paraphrase quotation.

> "In a middle-sized island, within a few decades, two massive changes altered fundamentally the accepted wisdom of the ages. In the Industrial revolution, craftworkers became irrelevant to the new economy. With the theory of evolution the creator-God of *Genesis* and Plato's Demiurge became irrelevant to the order of nature."

According to Darwin the natural species had no God-given permanence but were merely the latest adaptations in the very long march of mutations. According to Marx, the traditional forms of work, the age old crafts and professions, had no status either, apart from sentimental associations which would yield to the industrial order. Even more than the natural species, those forms of human specialization were provisional.

With both species and specialization, a sacramental understanding yielded to a calculus. Forms of work became merely the adaptations of a human collective to its environment in order to survive. Where a much more efficient adaptation appeared, it would be bound eventually to sweep all its competitors off the board. In Britain and France where the new steam powered modes of industrial production first appeared, their rulers and peoples had some choice concerning the change. But those nations which followed them had no real choice at all. Since the new system bankrupted all its competitors, they had to adopt it.

But did even the British have the freedom to choose in this matter? Or did the technology merely have to appear and the game was over? When Vespasian was rebuilding Rome after the year of the three emperors, he needed to move some large columns. An engineer on site put himself forward to do the work at very modest cost by means of a simple mechanical contrivance. Vespasian declined, saying that he had to provide work and wages for the laborers so they could put food on the table. But he sent the engineer away with a large and wholly unearned present. Even here the reason given is strictly social. There is nothing here to suggest that hauling columns is God-given. If those laborers had other means of buying their food such as the dole, would Vespasian have approved the contrivance of the engineer? Like the British, Vespasian had the choice. Unlike the British, he turned it down.

Is there any reason, as opposed to sentiment, for supposing that either the species or the forms of human specialization are God-given rather than more or less efficient adaptations in the cause of survival? In the case of the species there is the Romantic insistence on the beauty of creatures and their *joie-de-vivre*. In certain moments I feel that evolutionary theory as little explains the life around me as the phrase 'subsistence living' describes Louis XIV in Versailles. But this may just be a bad case of the pathetic fallacy. As for the forms of human specialization, Socrates is the best guide, whose reputation for wisdom came from his always talking of cobblers and carpenters. In the *Republic* he sets out the most fundamental work to be done: for shelter, food and apparel. And then he divides labor. But his divisions do not proceed from the demands of efficiency or social need. He divides labor according to differences he perceives in the range of human dispositions and propensities. He wants the work to suit the people in much if not all of their variety. This principle gives me the same lift as Jesus's remark that the Sabbath was made for man, not man for the Sabbath. This is why I think Plato lovable.

Between a society in which people earn their livings doing what they have a bent for, and a society in which they earn their livings otherwise, we must prefer the first. And we might still prefer it, however much wealth is added to the alternative. Here we have William Blake and John Ruskin, William Morris and Ananda Coomaraswamy. This was one debate in the nineteenth and twentieth centuries. But it is not the debate now. Socrates' theory in the *Republic* is conditional upon there being work for people to do. The question was merely how best to arrange this. People now in very large numbers need not work at all.

Is it better not to work than to work, all other things being equal? I think even factory workers would often choose to work. But surely in a workless society, those who wish to work are still free to do so. But hobbyists still need others as customers, students, audience. Which then is less free, a workless society in which many forms of work are quite redundant, and many are just hobbies, or a society in which one must work to live? This begins to sounds like a good question.

I think people need to serve others to be whole, and a workless society will inhibit the expression of that gratitude and devotion to others which work affords. So much for selflessness. But there is also a wonderful selfishness about work, and, indeed, about the species. In the beer-halls of Munich made infamous by Hitler there was a strange week-end rite. In those cavernous chambers, workers of all sorts would gather after their six days' labor and group themselves around tables according to their crafts and professions. Then, as the beer flowed from the steins, first one and then another would stand at the different tables and sing a rousing song in praise of his work and its superiority to all other occupations whatsoever. I imagine much cheering and foot-stamping from his immediate companions. This is an entirely apt and happy *esprit de corps*. And I am equally sure that each creature rejoices in being of its own kind and no other, and firmly believes that its particular form of life is the best one of them all. And it seeks to demonstrate this...

TUTOR

Good. I like that. You've certainly made something of the parallel between industrialization and the theory of evolution. Is that all you have to say directly about Plato's division of labor?

STUDENT

Yes, the rest of my essay is on 'Discuss the workless society.'

TUTOR

Let's stop here a moment and think about what you've just said. Plato, you think, is lovable because he divides labor to suit the different capacities for work which people have?

STUDENT

Yes.

TUTOR

But why should Plato suppose that suiting his citizens in this way will produce the workers his society needs? What if they all turned out to be potters or blacksmiths and not a farmer among them? They'd starve.

STUDENT

I thought about that and I think Plato thought the city-state was an organic entity in nature, just like an animal body. As the diet of a particular place nourishes all the organs in the body of an animal, so it sustains and produces all the kinds of people needed for a city there. The differentiation into distinct occupations within the collective corresponds to the differentiations of the food to make and sustain the various organs of the body.

TUTOR

Does Plato say that?

STUDENT

He has strange views about the origins of the classes from the earth with the different grades of metal in their souls, but he says that this is just a story to make them stick to their various occupations.

TUTOR

What about Socrates himself? What was his occupation?

STUDENT

His father owned a sculpture studio, and a sculpture of two Graces is traditionally attributed to Socrates. But he gave it all away and went on the streets.

TUTOR

Yes, I've always wondered how Socrates would have got on in Athens a couple of hundred years earlier, under Draco and Solon. Under both of them every Athenian male citizen had to account for himself every year before a magistrate, showing how he earned his living. Under Draco, failure in this brought the death penalty.

STUDENT

So what did Socrates live on? He was a hoplite, so he had to provide all his own armour and the rest.

TUTOR

Perhaps his armour was a bit old-fashioned. Good quality but out of date, because it was his father's old set. Like a charity boy in a private school.

STUDENT

Yes. The *Apology*'s like that. I just read it again and he seems less concerned to answer the charges than to say that he's been doing an important job of work here, as if to Draco or Solon. He's got a real chip on his shoulder.

TUTOR

Of course in his own republic Socrates would be a philosopher ruler and he says, doesn't he, that even if you don't live in his republic, you should live as if you do. And that's what he did and he annoyed the hell out of everyone. No wonder he claimed a state pension. But enough. You've still got some way to go before you've shown that Plato's occupations are not merely expedient but God-given. They may have appeared God-given to the ancients but how do you show that they actually were? And even if you could show this, how do you then demonstrate that these particular divisions of labor are the right ones, at precisely this or that degree of specialization?

STUDENT

I think Plato's pretty clear about the degree of specialization. Socrates prefers the simplest possible life style for his first citizens, so simple that his companions complain that he is describing a life fit only for pigs. These first citizens seem to spend most of their time singing hymns.

TUTOR

But have they got to the point in their city where they have specialized industries in particular quarters?

STUDENT

I don't know.

TUTOR

Because you don't know enough or because Plato is vague?

STUDENT

I can't remember anything about such arrangements in that first community.

TUTOR

Well, I think he's very vague about the occupations and people's predispositions to them. As he is, indeed, later in the *Republic* in his account of the ideas. Is he talking about the village blacksmith, or one in the blacksmiths' quarter of the city? It's never quite clear. Has everyone a predisposition for a particular form of work and only one? It all sounds very wishful. And what about gunsmiths and printers? Has the pattern of the innate human predispositions changed, mutated, to bring such people into existence? . . . Well, let us hear about the workless society?

Two Philosophy Tutorials

STUDENT

Once upon a time a magician summoned an elemental spirit to do the heavy work around his house. The giant rapidly cleaned and swept the house, dug the garden, mowed the lawns, cut the wood, brought the water and even washed, dried and ironed the clothes. But when the magician had no other orders to give, the elemental went crazy. Rushing into the town, he assaulted the citizens and smashed up the shops as a release for his energies. In his extremity, the magician went to the wizard who had been his teacher and asked for advice. His teacher replied 'set it to building a very high and strong flag-pole in your garden. When it has finished that and you have nothing else for it to do, just tell it to climb up and down the flagpole!'

I have heard this story used to illustrate the Hindu *Bhagavad Gita*. We are all born with arms and legs and the other human equipment, and we have to use it all even if life is only what you do when you can no longer sleep. But acts have consequences, so we must find something to do which has no bad consequences. The solution is to engage selflessly in the occupation to which you are called. And I must add that the Swami from whom I heard all this was deeply opposed to the caste system as it had devolved. So the furious energies of the elemental in the story represent that need to act in every human being. But of course, unlike elementals, human beings would not be happy climbing up and down a pole every day. Like elementals, on the other hand, humans may become violent if they have nothing to do.

So what do we do when we no longer work for pay but live instead on some dole and occupy ourselves as economically as we can with our domestic tasks? Some people may say that when this has become more normal and accepted as long term, the stigma largely disappears and the lack of a larger role ceases to hurt. Bread and circuses. But that dreadful Roman Colosseum did at least bring the mob together if only to witness cruelty. Where we are, the electronic devices which have displaced many from their work serve to isolate some of them still further physically, until each is linked only through a virtual world. Long before the new science of the Enlightenment, there was a very clear and widely shared analysis of self-inflicted human sadness. SOLITUDE + IDLENESS = MELAN-CHOLY. If this still applies, then the prospects for the new workless who live by the net are not good.

It is certainly surprising that there has not been a stronger response to the level of paid and unpaid worklessness already. Meanwhile economic self-sufficiency as a personal ideal continues to be promoted at every level. It may be, as you suggested, that evolutionary theory palliates the issue with the prospect of a massive human reorganization. Or the authority of our miraculous science retains our confidence despite all. And there is another possibility to be found in literature. It is well known that William Blake adopted a form of Satanism. He was the apostle of desire. For millennia religious and philosophical instruction had been devoted to the end of curbing desire, governing appetite, controlling the passions. Though Blake was a revolutionary in politics, he was profoundly traditional in his spiritual and moral life. And yet he was a Satanist. What had happened? He must have felt that in his time, human energy did not need restraint but stimulus, that the Londoners around him were mere ghosts of the people before them. And so his Christ who, like his devils, is energy supreme. We have hints of this 'poor, loveless, ever anxious crowd' in Wordsworth and Coleridge. Have the industrial and electronic revolutions occurred because of the peoples whose work they first made redundant and not despite them? It seems impossible when we consider the drive which has come from England to change the whole world. And then I think of Blake again, and even more of Tennyson with his strange rhapsodical languor at the very heart of Empire. And I think of that nineteenth century city of prostitutes which Dostoyevsky and Mayhew describe. I am very confused...

TUTOR

That's it?

STUDENT

Yes.

TUTOR

Well, it still seems a bit short but you write with a certain dash, so we'll say it just seems short.

STUDENT

Thank you.

TUTOR

And I liked the Socratic ending. Now you've said a bit about Plato and about worklessness, but you've hardly spoken of automation. So, tell me, what is the machine?

STUDENT

A labor-saving contrivance?

TUTOR

Isn't that a tool, too? So what's the difference between a tool and a machine? Don't think of things, think of uses.

STUDENT

I don't understand.

TUTOR

We would say that a piano was a tool for a concert pianist, but that a pianola or player-piano or music-box was a machine?

STUDENT

I think so.

TUTOR

Well, how about a pocket calculator with a battery? For a surveyor or engineer making complex calculations at work, the calculator would be a tool. But for a fifteen year old who can hardly multiply seven by five, it's more like a machine.

STUDENT

All right.

TUTOR

So what is the difference between a tool and a machine?

STUDENT

A tool extends the power and range of a faculty in the person who uses it. A machine replaces the human faculty in part or whole.

TUTOR

Close enough. Now, is there any reason why we should use our faculties rather than not use them, all other things being equal?

STUDENT

I think we should use them.

TUTOR

I asked for a reason.

STUDENT

Er... If you've got it, flaunt it! Use it or lose it!

TUTOR

Do you know Aristotle's definition of pleasure as 'unhindered activity'? The proper exercise of any faculty or organ in its healthy state is unhindered activity and so far it is pleasant. And this is true of pleasures which are preceded by needs and of pure pleasures which come to us without any preceding discomfort, like the unexpected scent of a rose in clear air.

STUDENT

And that's a good reason for exercising a faculty?

TUTOR

Well, it might be if it was a good definition of pleasure.

STUDENT

But what about smelling nasty smells or hearing ugly sounds? That's not pleasant.

TUTOR

True, but here the unpleasantness of noise or smell outweighs the pleasantness of the hearing or smelling and hinders them.

STUDENT

So in and of itself the unhindered exercise of any faculty or organ is pleasant?

TUTOR

Yes, think of a good shit.

STUDENT

Well, yes, I see. And you're saying that if automation replaces the exercise of human faculties which give pleasure, this is wrong.

TUTOR

No, just less pleasant in this respect and to this degree. After further consideration in any particular instance, we might say that automation here was not merely less pleasant than what it replaced in this respect and to this degree, but less pleasant overall. But let's try it another way. How do craftworkers exercise their faculties as opposed to factory hands?

STUDENT

But that's not the situation we're facing with worklessness?

TUTOR

No, but we're talking automation.

STUDENT

OK... Well, the craftworkers often have to design what is to be made, but the factory hand performs a ready-made task. Oh! I see. You're talking about that other passage from Plato in the hand-out where the carpenter looks to the idea of the bed in the mind of God and then copies it.

TUTOR

Yes.

STUDENT

So the difference between craftworker and factory worker is that the craftworker has an insight into the mind of God?

TUTOR

That's how it's often put. The crafts and professions are active and practical but they are all contemplative too.

STUDENT

So what's this looking into the mind of God?

TUTOR

It's difficult, especially as a few pages on, Socrates say that it is not the craftworker but the client, the customer, who knows most about the artefact desired... So, again, how do craftworkers differ from factory hands?

STUDENT

They are contemplative.

TUTOR

And how do craftworkers and factory hands differ from the workless?

STUDENT

They are active.

TUTOR

All right. Now, how important is it that those people, like the craftworker, who are capable of designing actually do design?

STUDENT

I can see that they are creative but I'm not at all sure about the mind of God.

TUTOR

Now, this is fascinating. For Plato human artefacts are in nature just like spiders' webs and birds' nests, indeed just like spiders and birds. He has not yet made the distinction between natural and artificial which we make. So a bed is in the mind of God in exactly the same way that a horse or an oak-tree is.

STUDENT

So, after all, craftworkers are just the factory hands of God with a ready-made task.

TUTOR

A noble status! And if it comes to that, I'm not at all sure, being married, that I'd want to buy a bed from anyone who had contemplated the idea of the bed in the mind of God when making my bed.

STUDENT

I'm sorry?

TUTOR

Well, the craftsman God for Athens was Hephaestus, and he did indeed make a bed of which we hear. Homer tells us that on this bed Hephaestus caught his wife Aphrodite and the God Ares cuckolding him. See what I mean, any bed made by contemplating that bed is bound to be ill-omened. But our time is nearly up. One last question: if you were the Government what, if anything, would you do about worklessness?

STUDENT

I don't know. Of course I've thought about it. Who hasn't? I think I would encourage open markets. I don't mean international free trade, but stalls outdoors or under shedding. I'm very attracted to the work of the Prince's School and his traditional village. I think we should practise all our traditional crafts and agriculture and preserve that way of life as a model if our hypersophistication collapses. So I would greatly increase opportunities for the study and practice of the crafts which work with wood, clay metal, leather, textiles and so on. I would certainly restore the Hunt for its animal husbandry. And I would introduce traditional modes of market gardening on a large scale. But I don't think we should evangelize. The Anglos have made enough difference to the world as it is.

TUTOR

And what about you? What will you do when you graduate?

STUDENT

Try to get a paid teaching post. If I can't, I've got my certificates in plumbing and roofing.

TUTOR

Clever.

STUDENT

And you?

TUTOR

My contract ends at the end of next year and after that I don't know. It doesn't look good. I've had a fine run and we've plenty to live on. At worst I'll finish writing up conversations like this. I have to say that I grieve when I think my grandchildren won't be paid to do what we've done here. As a College and a university college we've taught philosophy for over forty years, but no more. And no more, I think, for many others as electronic technology replaces the lecture-room. But, of course, I'm not talking as a scholar here or a grand-parent, just another self interested rent-seeker.

A Dialogue on Eternity

A

Here's an old argument about space and time:

First premise: There is an adequate explanation for everything.

Second premise: The world we see in front of us could just as well be its mirror image, with left and right exchanged. There can be no explanation for why it is one way round rather than the other.

Conclusion: The world is not one way round rather than the other. Space is not a permanent pre-existing place in which the world is set. Space is not absolute in this way.

A similar argument applies to time. There can be no explanation for why the universe came into existence when it did, rather than a billion years before or after. Therefore it did not come into existence when it did. No more than space is time a permanent, pre-existent continuum in which the world is set. Space is an arrangement of places, as time is of events.

B

Nonetheless, each and every person occupies a unique series of positions within a single space-time continuum common to us all.

A

Whose space-time continuum, the spherical geographer's, the flat-earther's or the Einsteinian relativist's?

B

It doesn't matter which one it is. We all see the same one. Blake says:

A fool sees not the same tree that a wise man sees.

But, of course, there has to be the one tree there which they both see if we are to compare and contrast their views of it.

A

Perhaps we share an external world as you say. We certainly share an inner spirit. For us there is no perceiving of a shared external world, if there is one, except through some shared language.

B

Perhaps, but this we can say. Every sight of the world is a marriage, however momentary, between what is out there to be seen and who is seeing it. Each partner in this marriage is changing every moment, so no two perceptions are ever quite the same. Nonetheless, there is something other than the perceiver in an act of perceiving the world. That is Blake's tree. And so it is quite impossible that the whole of any one's experience in space and time is equal to the whole of what is in the space and time which they experience.

A

You distinguished between what is out there to be seen and who is seeing it, as if you could have any clue at all about this other partner in the marriage besides ourselves. You suppose it to be some sort of external world common to us all. But, really, you were only distinguishing between what we see and what we think we see. What we see is almost always far more visually complex than we bother to notice. And sometimes our expectations are brought to nothing by brute fact, as when I put my foot down on a stair which is not there. Neither of these observations is evidence of an external world, but only that I have experiences of which I am not fully conscious. It is not an external world but my own experience which eludes me. There is almost always a gap between that wonderful experience and my stupid apprehension of it. These are the sadly ill-matched partners in your marriage. In the same way dreams are wonderful and elude our dreaming selves, but they do not entail that their worlds exist externally.

B

People don't dream of the same tree together. Now they may, I suppose, experience the same tree from their different physical and mental perspectives because God has put a direct vision of the tree into the minds of each one of them. But, then, what does it mean to talk of the same tree? Surely it is more reasonable to suppose that there is an external world where there is the one tree which they all see?

A

Most Westerners think nowadays that the universe was once lifeless, at least around this tiny corner of it. Then creatures somehow appeared which perceived the world from which they emerged. Time and space, like money, have been fantastically inflated in the last century. But try it this way round. The purpose of the creation is the bringing of the fool and the wise man together for the edification of one and the sanctification of the other. For this, their sharing of a common world about which to discourse is essential. What you call the external world is merely the fulfilment of the conditions which have to be met for such discourse to be possible. And the first such condition is a shared universe almost too wonderful to know.

B

That is a massive confusion of cause and effect.

A

How? On the one side we have a universe with a certain history. On the other side we have a fool, a wise man and a tree. Which of these two states of affairs brought about the other, whether either or neither, is quite indeterminable scientifically. Spiritual people view all the world's wonders as means to spiritual ends. The physical world is one of the lessons we learn with others who share it with us. It is altogether a most cunning device. But after the lesson is learnt, there is no residue. We are all taken up into heaven, but we do not leave an empty world behind. The physical heavens themselves, we are told in one scripture, will be rolled up like a scroll, as they were created out of nothing in the first place.

B

You cannot be serious when you say that this whole universe exists simply so that a fool and a wise man should see a tree!

A

That tree, for Blake, is Christ's cross, and Christians have always taken it very seriously in just the way I have described. Not long ago everyone believed that, and not the materialist's view. Scientifically, the crucifixion and resurrection were the central events of history. Nowadays Science is non-teleological in principle, if not always in practice. It adopts this point of view for methodological reasons and proceeds from there. But it has no way of determining whether the creation does serve some purpose, spiritual or otherwise. It adopts the hypothesis that there is no purpose, but it does not and cannot and is not concerned to prove it.

✤

A

When I think 'I am here at my desk this Tuesday morning', I am aware that I am not somewhere else. I have to be more or less aware of somewhere else to give any sense to my thinking that I am here now. My largest understanding of that somewhere else is all the places and times with which I am acquainted directly or through reproductions, and all the places and times of which I have merely heard. It is against this that I set my sense of here and now. But this largest somewhere else is still within my cognizance. It is the sense of the universe which I happen to have, and it is composed of my memories of what I have experienced and what I have heard.

Memories come in two kinds at least. There are those that I conjure as best I can at will. These memories I see and understand from where I am now. And there are memories which are unbidden or forgotten, but which can burst upon the mind with a sense that I am experiencing the event remembered from the same point of view from which it was originally experienced, as a nine-year-old child, say. Wordsworth was very concerned with this second class of memories.

Suppose now a phase or state of mind in which all of these memories of the second kind are present simultaneously and in full by the merest turning of attention; each memory evoking the innumerable others which had contributed to its forms and feelings. When we remember usually, we focus and isolate the memory, but in this state of consciousness the whole of memory seems to be present. For each memory is seen to be what it is only by virtue of its place in the whole, like a palaeontologist's recreation of a dinosaur from a sliver of bone. Each memory brings its own cascade of the memories which helped to form it and each of them likewise and on and on. This is a solitary experience since it requires a fuller attention than ever before, but it is not in the least a solipsistic one. What I had heard from others would then play a much larger part even than my own encounters in the making of that universe. And all the memories would be bound together by the common language in which I have always had to think. It is very clear in this exaltation that every human mind is potentially just the same, has to be to experience and remember as it does every moment of the day. The exaltation is our normal state because it is at last a proper awareness of what each of us is in every single moment of our waking lives. It is so intimate and immediate a realization that it would be silly even to call it a discovery. Allah is as close as the jugular vein, I have heard it said. And yet, somehow, the great world is now within me, and my life and safety stand entirely above and beyond it for the first time ever.

B

It all sounds very wonderful but I find it hard to believe that you remember every time you shaved or washed your hands even in that state of consciousness. And I am not clear about how other peoples' experiences enter into your own. Are you saying that your experiences and other people's are identical?

A

You are quite right to raise both these difficulties, and I am going to suggest a way in which they could be resolved together. First, I am sure you would accept that in the case of an original and the images of it, knowledge of the original confers a certain grasp of all its copies. Take Botticelli's *Primavera* in the Uffizi in Florence. If you have seen that, you have effective knowledge of all its likenesses and reproductions. Perhaps, then, the feeling in that state of consciousness that all the occasions of my washing are within my recall has less to do with my actually recalling them, or even so many of them as would confuse me, but rather with a grasping of the experience principially or originally in some way. That is, what would explain that feeling of total recall is a theory of ideas, of eternal entities which cause all the phenomena as originals project their images. And those eternal ideas are the objects of a common or universal intellect in which we all share at the highest levels of our souls. In the eternal state I have described, these ideas are known directly as eternal, causal and universal among thinking beings. 'The idea of washing', for example, if not shaving.

B

Let me see if I understand you. You are saying that you have experienced eternity, where by eternity you mean the timeless plenum of all events. But when pressed. you admit that you did not then experience even the plenum of your own doings to that point, and you invoked some theory of ideas of which you then had more direct knowledge. Now whether we ascend with Plato from the ideas to eternity, or we descend with you from eternity to the 'ideas.' I am not persuaded. And as for this common intellect and its universal objects, I feel as though I'm back in Cordoba with Averroës.

A

You are forgetting that I began all this with the word 'suppose.' And you are also forgetting that we began with a hypothetical experience, a thought-experiment it is true, but as of an actual experience. You have yourself remembered Averroës, and the claim to have experienced eternity is by no means uncommon, especially in antiquity and the middle ages. I must say that though I respect your questioning of my theory of ideas, I do hope that you do not reject those experiences of eternity, since they are very well attested. And the long history of philosophy and theology is largely built on them!

B

And I, in my turn, said only that I was not persuaded. But I am engaged. Somehow I do know what you are saying, and I cannot quite see how a sceptic should!

A

Well, in that case I must tell you that you understand me all too well, and that your questions have been entirely to the point. And that is something, when we consider both my feeble apperceptions of such states of consciousness, and the laborious problems which beset our common language about them. Still, I seem to have a follower here in the only sense that matters.

🌴

B

Let me return to how a person's identity depends upon their spatio-temporal continuity. From my understanding of what you have said, that limited identity is still part of the eternity revealed in the exaltation. Indeed, it must be since all those experiences which are experienced in that limited identity comprise the plenum of memories now experienced simultaneously. Each of those memories is of an experience in time, by a person in time. So both our eternal and our temporal identities are strictly necessary even on your account. At best, you seem to hold the theory that each of us has two identities.

A

One way to think of it is to suppose that these two identities are lovers bound together in a most passionate embrace. For if 'eternity is in love with the productions of time', it is no less true, as I have said, that our experience of every moment in time involves, more or less distantly, the entirety of our experiences up to that moment. In most people, these two identities in their embrace are both asleep. Anyone who supposes that their whole identity consists only in their spatio-temporal continuity has very little sense of what is involved even in that. But when the two identities wake up, their love-play is something to behold.

B

Even so, it seems that your eternity requires that sense of identity which is our awareness of our spatio-temporal continuity in the world. That is our plain, old being here of which I am still more sure than anything else. So it seems that your Nirvana is the opposite of the one in which many Buddhists believe. For they believe Nirvana cannot be gained before death, but your eternity seems to require a living person in the world to experience it, or at least a person with all the memories of a living person.

A

But why see it from the point of view of time rather than eternity? Of course, if anyone sees eternity here in the world, they see it as a living person at a certain time and place before, during and after. And they see it clothed, as it were, in their own memories. Who knows how eternity would be without such trappings? Here again a theory of ideas may play a part. But from the point of view of eternity, that spatio-temporal continuum is actually a *totum simul* now. Standing in eternity, there can be no before and after death because there is no before and after. Standing there, it cannot even be said that this exaltation is new, even though it is a revelation. It is closer than ever before to what is there always. The difference is only in the awareness. But with the awareness comes a certainty that that old sense of the spatio-temporally continuous self is a misunderstanding, not least because of its fear of death as annihilation. In this way the two identities are not equals or contraries. The eternal trumps the temporal at every point. The temporal identity exists for the consummation of that love-making. Eternity is a female black widow spider who destroys her mate, the identity in space and time, as soon as he has fertilized her, then eats the corpse. That is how dead our identity in space and time feels after the encounter.

B

Well, perhaps, but I am not sure I would enjoy even the exaltation. I know the experience which you described before, of remembering something forgotten and unbidden from the very point of view from which I had experienced it as a child. I found that rush of memories, that lost but rapidly reconstituting world, rather disconcerting. I cannot imagine what it would be like if that process went on and on. Even the thought of it is vertiginous.

A

But, of course, it has entirely its own stability, much more rocklike than the one on which our spatio-temporal continuity depends. I will go further and say that the stability of the spatio-temporal continuum is itself an effect of a much steadier eternity. Eternity is stable because it is inviolable. Including everything in time and space, it is unassailable by anything in time and space. And it has its own equilibrium in other ways, of a much more substantial kind than our poor globe and cosmos. It is here that is vertiginous, the so-called real world. Blake used to talk of returning to the abyss of the five senses.

B

Well, once again, I remain to be persuaded, and I would like to be persuaded because I have understood enough of what you have said to be unsettled, if not convinced.

A

I am not sure that I want to convince you, as if this were a position in a debate. I said before that to be aware of my being here now, I must be aware to some extent of all the other times and places I might be. The same is true of any judgement. Any proposition about a state of affairs in the world gains its force from all the propositions it denies, as well as from all its corollaries. It carries those other propositions with it as the background against which it is set. It follows from this that to understand any such proposition requires an understanding of all those other propositions related to it negatively and positively. So when we affirm a proposition we are tacitly affirming all its negations as possible beliefs, though in the very act of contradicting them. But if we see that, we see that holding one such opinion of all those possible ones, when they all have to be in the mind, is self-defeating. And so too with the virtues and vices. They all demand each other in principle and so there is a necessary coincidence of each in all the others and of all the others in each. The thing becomes utterly indivisible, even the least and worst of it. And so it is redeemed and made perfect. But there is one thing even more perfect than all this, and that is anything which can help us to achieve it. Which is why the poets and preachers and scholars labor.

Plato Jokes[1]

I N THE HISTORY AND THEORY of art Plato is very well known
for his attacks on representational art and for his exclusion of
poets from his ideal republic. In fact, Plato was not opposed to
representational art nor to poetry. The story of how this mistake
came to be made is a salutary one for readers of Plato. The story
reveals just how playful and paradoxical his dialogues can be.

Plato was born during Athens' democratic heyday in the later 5th
century BC and was himself a poet to whom many fine lyrics are
traditionally attributed. But then, some say, he met Socrates who
persuaded him to change his ways and Plato took to writing prose
dialogues in which Socrates is usually the main speaker.[2] In the
greatest of these dialogues, the *Republic*, Socrates sets out his vision
of personal and social justice and he attacks poetry and drama of
various kinds. Socrates argued that the poetry taught in his time,
Homer and the others, had bad effects on his fellow citizens.[3]

Plato's Socrates attacks Homer and Hesiod for describing the
Gods as lying, cheating and committing adultery. Hesiod had told
the story of how Cronus had castrated his own father Uranus.[4]
Again, Homer often showed his heroes cracking under pressure and
these were poor examples for the young. In the *Iliad* Homer
describes at length the cunning of Agamemnon, the Commander in
Chief. But, Socrates says, if Homer really knew anything about generalship, his fellow citizens would not have let him languish as a
poet. Good generals were much greater assets to a city than poets,
but Homer was good only at appearing to know about generalship.

1. This article was first published by the *Temenos Academy Review*, whom the
author gratefully acknowledges for permission to reprint it.
2. For example: Diogenes Laertius, III.5.
3. *Republic*, 376e–392c.
4. Hesiod, *Theogony*, 178–182.

Then Socrates turns to the Athenian tragedies. Like Homer the tragedians are illusionists. Their productions bear the same relation to the scenes which they represent as paintings do. For Socrates an actor acting a part in a play is a bare image of a person. And what do we want with images of people and things when we have the reality all round us? But Socrates hated the tragedies above all for their vileness. They retold on the stage the most horrible tales of incest, child murder, patricide and insanity. In Socrates' view these plays enacted the fantasies of tyrants and psychopaths.[5] And, of course, it is from these same plays that Freud derived his knowledge and his names of the complexes. For Socrates, such nightmares are best treated by a quiet period before going to sleep and an improving book. He does not deny them, note. But he believes that giving them any more room than you have to is a hellish mistake.

Socrates personally had some uncomfortable encounters with dramatic poets. The comic playwright Aristophanes put on a play about Socrates, the *Clouds*, which caricatured him as a flea-ridden, money-grubbing shyster. While the play was being performed, Socrates is said to have stood up in the middle of the large audience, to help strangers to the city recognize him because he was very different in the flesh from the grotesque who was playing him on stage.[6] In the *Apology* he mentions the damage which the play had done to his reputation.[7]

So it is not much of a surprise when at the start of *Republic X* Socrates says to his companions

> 'You know, among all the excellent features of our ideal state, there's none I rank higher than its treatment of poetry.'
> 'Why, exactly?'
> 'Because it excluded all representation.'[8]

This comment, and what Socrates has said and now says about poetry and drama, have branded Socrates and Plato as enemies of

---

5. *Republic*, 571 c–d.
6. Aelian, *Variae Historiae*, II.13.
7. *Apology*, 19 b–c.
8. *Republic*, 595a, tr. H. D. P. Lee, Penguin, 1987.

the open society, as friends of repression and state censorship. Whatever damage was done to poetry and drama by Socrates' attacks, they have done far more damage to Socrates and Plato, certainly in our age.

But this view of Socrates' comment misses a single startling fact. The comment is itself made by a character in a dramatic dialogue, by a character who historically would not have wanted to be there. I think Socrates had every justification for stepping off Plato's stage and saying he wanted no part of it. Some rich boy, whose notion of wisdom was rudimentary, chose to write a literary life of this man who had devoted himself to real wisdom! This, I think, is how Plato imagined Socrates' response.[9] This was the great difference between Plato and his teacher: Socrates wrote no dialogues. Did he read any of Plato's? I can hear the modest but penetrating disclaimers and Plato's voice urging his reasons. So yes, for a character in a dramatic dialogue struggling to escape his predicament, I can see that a critique of representation would have a very special appeal. With his infamous comment, Socrates does no more than stand up in the theatre again, but this time his gesture is an active protest.

A great artist meets a great man. The artist says 'I am nothing to the greatness of this man and I can show nothing of him.' And he has the man himself say it. With his comment, Socrates tells us how happy he would be to escape his hagiographer's limits. As for me, I like dramatic dialogues, especially ones with Socrates. Especially ones by Plato. None of this bears upon Plato's views of poetry. It is a purely personal issue between two friends. It is hard not to side with Socrates until we remember what we would lose if he won.

The practice of dramatic representation is condemned by Plato's dramatic representation of Socrates. How can we possibly believe in this? It is like the famous liar paradox: all Cretans are liars; I am a Cretan; therefore I am a liar. But my being a liar vitiates anything I say, though not the logic of my syllogism. According to Bertrand Russell, such paradoxes arise when a term of the second order, such as 'liar', is introduced. For the term 'liar' here is self-referential in respect of such speech acts as the one in which it now appears. In

---

9. Cf. Diogenes Laertius, III. 35c.

the same way, the fact that dramatic representation is here being condemned by a dramatic representation undermines the condemnation. At the most we can say that Plato in his practice and Socrates in his arguments disagree about the value of dramaturgy.

Plato was close in his art to Aristophanes and loved a crazy story. Under the pillow of Plato's death bed was found a copy of Aristophanes' comedies.[10] There is the story of the bisected giants which Plato gives to Aristophanes in the *Symposium*.[11] In the last pages of the *Timaeus* we learn exactly how the way we have lived our human lives determines the lives to follow. Non-theoretical astronomers become birds, appetitive souls become quadrupeds and sink on down through the hierarchy of lives until they finish as snakes and fish.[12] In the *Statesman* we learn of the reverse cycles of time when people are born out of the ground bent, wrinkled and white-haired and grow younger as the years pass. Those born at the time of a cyclical change are born white-haired and grow younger and then suddenly the process reverses and they start to grow old again.[13] All these stories would make scripts for Aristophanes' comic fantasies. What Plato gives us here is continuous in his art with the myths at the ends of *Phaedo, Republic* and *Gorgias*.

I see no reason to suppose that Plato wrote all his poems as a young man and then gave away the practice. This theory may spring from the common misreading of Plato's own views of art which we have seen. Plato made contributions to Greek letters with his poems and with certain theorems concerning the mathematics of the square. His dialogues are full of mathematics and poetry and are themselves the most poetic of all the extended philosophies which we have. But his greatest achievement was the crafting of his leading character. Socrates is the first hero of the west to appear in a series. In writing the dialogues Plato differed greatly from Socrates who did no such thing. In justice to both of them Plato dramatized their difference. And so he took an advantage: the last and only word. But

10. Olmpiodorus, *Commentary on the First Alcibiades of Plato*, 2.69.
11. *Symposium*, 189–193.
12. *Timaeus*, 90 d–92 c.
13. *Statesman*, 27 2–3.

Plato gave his Socrates so strong a case against dramaturgy that we have supposed it to be Plato's too, a ridiculous notion.

In the *Phaedo* Plato really did have the last word. In prison Socrates has been turning the fables of Aesop into verse. All his life, Socrates says, a dream has told him to study the arts. He had hoped his dialectic would be enough, but now at the crunch he is covering all his bases.[14]

🌴

Plato is playful. There is humor on almost every page. This creates problems for the interpreter since the joke is often the point of a statement. For the most part the jokes are logical as with the contradiction between Socrates as representation and Socrates on representation. But the real difficulty for the interpreter comes from Plato's taste for the absurd. In the *Protagoras* Socrates is the narrator and he guys Protagoras at every turn, especially the precise choric dance of the master's attendants as they accompany but never precede him in his pacing of the portico. Protagoras tells Socrates that there have always been Sophists in Greece but that previously they had to operate *incognito* for fear of malice and persecution. But he, Protagoras, believed that openness was a better protection than secrecy and called himself what he actually was.[15] And so, according to Protagoras, Homer and Hesiod and all the wise men of Greece were just like Protagoras in being Sophists but he was the first to declare himself.

Socrates listens to this and much else and when his turn to speak comes, he refers to these claims of Protagoras and protests that Protagoras did not go far enough. Socrates claims in addition that Sparta owes its good government and high reputation to the Sophists and no one else. This claim of Socrates was counter-intuitive to a degree, because Sparta was famous for its dislike of fine speeches and its distrust of foreign ways. Sparta was the very type of the reactionary and conservative city. But Socrates suggests the reason why the Spartans had their regular purgings of the city and expelled all

14. *Phaedo*, 60d–61b.
15. *Protagoras*, 316–317.

the foreigners was to establish perfect security and secrecy. In the lock-down they could consort openly with their Sophists and still keep the real reason for their extraordinary success from the rest of Greece.[16]

This is fatuous and it is meant to be. But it is no more fatuous that Protagoras' claims that all the wise men of Greece were Sophists but did not call themselves so for fear of persecution. This is the logic from which conspiracy theory grows. Why did the elephant paint its toenails purple? To hide in a grape-vine. Well, have you ever seen an elephant hiding in a grape-vine? That's because painting its toenails is a very successful manoeuvre. Socrates cannot call Protagoras on his absurd claims about the wisest of the Greeks because Protagoras has already covered himself. He has made the additional claim that they hid the fact that they were Sophists out of fear. What Socrates does instead is to demonstrate the absurdity by using the same kind of argument to prove a manifest nonsense.

But all this occurs near the start of Socrates' speech and we are given no indication of the audience's reaction. When Socrates ends his speech and asks Protagoras that they return to their discussions about virtue, Protagoras does not respond until the others all press him. Socrates' play with Protagoras' grandiloquent claim about Sophists is subtle and also disrespectful. Protagoras has said that he is old enough to be the father of everyone present. Socrates does not meet him directly in his claims about the Sophists of old. He mimics him, but he pads his equally absurd claims with specious details to give them a superficial plausibility. There is this measure of tact in Socrates' behavior towards Protagoras. But Protagoras is still the old king confronting humiliation at the hands of his more agile successor.

🌴

In one most notable instance of Platonic humor there was absolutely no tact at all. And this tactlessness earned Socrates the death sentence. The whole of Socrates' defence is rather tactless as Plato gives it to us. Socrates begins by telling his five hundred jurors that

16. *Protagoras*, 342–343.

he will not be addressing them as some defendants did, begging and weeping and parading their children. He will be speaking to them as he always had and at one point he puts one of his accusers, Meletus, through some standard Socratic refutations, of the kind to be found everywhere in the accounts of Plato and Xenophon. He tells his jurors that they need not tell him that he could leave the court a free man provided that he agreed to stop bothering people with his questions. He had been sent to ask those questions by the God Apollo himself and only He could countermand that vocation.[17]

The jurors confer and arrive at a verdict of guilty by a narrow margin. The law was that at this point the convicted person nominate an appropriate penalty. When Socrates nominates his penalty he suggests that in the circumstances a state pension for life would be appropriate, given his poverty and his service to the state. For, he says, he has done Athens much more good than any Olympic victor ever did. To be sure, at the end of this short speech he dismounts from his high horse and proposes that he be fined a mina. His friends contribute and their proposal is a fine of thirty mina.

In the context of his conviction Socrates' proposal of a state pension for himself is outrageous. Those to whom this story is told for the first time invariably smile at least and usually laugh. So it is humorous enough at some level, perhaps simply for the rapidity of the shift from punishment to reward. The shock of the contrary here occasions a physical spasm. But there can be no doubt at all that none of those jurymen in their high seriousness found Socrates' proposal in the least amusing. Many must have seen it as a deliberate and flagrant insult to themselves, the Athenian democracy, the law and the Gods themselves. From this point of view Socrates' proposal was an error of judgement. When at the end of this short speech Socrates changes tack and proposes a small fine, it may be that he has caught some sense from his jurors that his proposal so far is a bad mistake.

A bad mistake but nothing worse than that in Socrates' view. Even if he has provoked them to sentence him to death, that is of much less importance to Socrates than whether or not he has acted justly. After

---

17. *Apology,* 29 a–c.

being sentenced to death Socrates tells his supporters on the jury that the little voice which always told him not to do something when he was on the point of doing the wrong thing, had been completely silent that day.[18] So it must have been silent when he proposed his pension. And the shift from punishment to pension is really no more extraordinary than the tenor of his whole defence where he claims that the actions of which he stands accused are his devotions to Apollo and were sanctioned by the God himself. He compares his duty to Apollo to a soldier's duty on the battle field. Socrates' day in court was his opportunity to spell out the meaning of an exemplary life and he took it as he never had before. From Socrates' point of view there was nothing humorous about his proposal. He was calling it just as he saw it, as he had throughout his speech.

I have a serious reservation about Socrates' actions here which I have rarely seen raised. It seems that it does not matter very much to Socrates whether his jury convict him or even sentence him to death. The line of his defence and his proposing a pension for himself may be strictly accurate and reasonable from his point of view but they are both highly provocative. By this stage of his career Socrates was a very sophisticated reader of audiences, so he must have known how provocative he was. Now, morally, to have played a part in the killing of Socrates was much worse than to die as Socrates. But only if Socrates played no part in his being killed. Still, the same has been said of Jesus before Pilate, and Jesus was conspicuously silent. So whether an honest defence or silence, the outcome is likely to be the same. Was Socrates 'hungry for an imagined martyrdom', to use John Donne's phrase for Catholic recalcitrants? In that case Anytus and Meletus bear a lighter load than Ananias and Caiaphas. For then Anytus and Meletus become Socrates' unwitting accomplices in a crime against himself.

I have no sense of any such reservation in Socrates from what he says, nor in Plato from the way in which he has composed his courtroom drama. Socrates steers near the edge with his jurors much of the time. He is a man who can at last say what he has long had a mind to say but could not, because his little voice forbade it. He is

18. *Apology*, 40 a–c.

not talking to the jurors as he has talked to the Athenians all his life. He is much ruder than usual in his dialectical refutations of Meletus, and there are none of the modest disclaimers and gentle ironies about his mission we find everywhere in the Dialogues. Now he is the servant of God revealed, and his mission is the greatest benefit Apollo has ever bestowed on Athens. Socrates knows very well the precise legal conditions under which he is speaking and how his limited time cannot be interrupted. For him and for us his speech is a catharsis and that is why the proposal for the pension is so mirth-provoking. It neatly caps all the relief we have already felt from this plain speaking, by going one outrageous step further. For, of course, it is a proposal we agree with entirely.

It is a very elevated speech even for Plato. Socrates invites the reader to enjoy a point of view in which ones own death is a matter of minor consequence compared to living wrongly. So radical is this belief in him that he has devoted his entire life to finding out how to live rightly. The perspective on his neighbors, jurors and accusers that this point of view gave Socrates was highly eccentric but completely coherent and consistent. It shapes almost everything in his speech. And so we see what most of his jurors cannot see. But at the same time we also see why they cannot see it, how provocative he is and how galling to their pride and political beliefs. And by the end, when Socrates says goodbye, we know exactly how right his little voice was to hold off on this occasion, despite any reservation we may have about the harm he may have done his jurors by provoking them. Plato succeeds in encapsulating a whole life in one speech which converts Socrates from a gadfly of the Athenians to a gadfly of the world.

There is one last possibility. Let us suppose that Plato's Socrates makes a sincere if outspoken attempt to defend himself against the charges he faces. He is convicted by a small majority. But that conviction, whatever the penalty, is fatal to his mission. He will no longer be able to interrogate the citizenry. Like the carpenter in the *Republic* who falls sick, he is happy to die if he can no longer work.[19] And so, at this point and not before, Socrates pushes them

---

19. *Republic*, 406 d–e.

into it with his proposal for a pension. How culpable is Socrates here of committing suicide-by-court? It is a very simple solution to the pointlessness of the rest of his life, and his jurymen are now committed. He owes nothing at all to those who have condemned and prohibited his divine mission, though he is still careful to exonerate those of them who are guiltless.

✿

The last of these four Platonic jokes comes, like the first, from the *Republic*. If we ask what is the guiding principle of Socrates' ideal state, one answer is his theory of the division of labor, the principle that each of us is naturally fitted for one kind of work rather than others. This principle is clearly and distinctly stated early in the discussion of the ideal constitution, just two or three pages after that discussion begins. As always in the dialectic, each step of the argument is set out as a separate proposition in the most exposed and vulnerable manner possible. Socrates and Adeimantus have agreed that their fledgling state will need four or five citizens and Socrates has asked whether each of these citizens should do everything for himself or whether each should practise one craft and all share the products of their various labors.

To this question Adeimantus replies that perhaps sharing would be the easier of the two choices. Socrates says

> It would not, by Zeus, be at all strange, for now that you have mentioned it, it occurs to me myself that, to begin with, our several natures are not all alike but different. One man is naturally fitted for one task, and another for another. Don't you think so?[20]

Adeimantus agrees. Then Socrates lists several practical reasons why the dividing of labor is a more efficient way of getting work done. From this theory of natural aptitudes will emerge the theory of the four social classes, and from them the elaborate theories of education which are the bulk of the book. From this same theory of natural aptitudes comes the historical theory towards the end of the

---

20. *Republic,* 370 a–b, tr.: Paul Shorey, *Plato Collected Dialogues*, Bollingen, 1996.

Republic, according to which power devolves from the highest to the lowest classes through an internal struggle over many centuries. And the *Republic* defines justice, the object of its search, as doing our own work without interfering in anyone else's.

If then we had to nominate just one turning point in the argument of the *Republic* this moment might very well be our choice. Socrates himself is moved to exclaim 'By Zeus!' as if it was only while Adeimantus was replying that he realized how important the issue was. He has just at that moment had a brainwave or a startling insight. So Plato highlights the moment when this crucial element in his theory is introduced. But, of course, if Socrates has only just now realized how important the division of labor is, it follows that his ideal constitution, his theory of education, his historical analysis and his definition of justice are all of them made up on the spot.

With Socratic irony in general I have no problem. His claim to know nothing seems to me quite compatible with his skilful refutations in the early Dialogues. To claim honestly that one knows nothing requires an enormous amount of work. One must study all that has been claimed as knowledge and be able to show that it falls short. Sceptics are very learned people, and they have precisely the skills which Socrates demonstrates. Again, it seems to me quite reasonable for Socrates to claim that he does not know whether a theory or definition presented to him is true until he has tested it. Socrates seems to think that all language shares the precision of geometry, and in geometry the truth or falsity of a proposition may not be at all obvious without systematic investigation. So he may reasonably claim not to know whether a given proposition is true without testing it. It is true that his refutations are astonishingly economical and acute, however.

But Socrates' pretence that his fundamental principle in the *Republic* had only just come to him on the spur of the moment entails all his other teaching on the state in the *Republic* is spontaneous too. To some degree this preserves Socrates' claims to ignorance. What he has to say in the *Republic* is impromptu, improvised, off the top of his head. He is merely exploring certain possibilities as they strike him during the course of the discussion. The problem arises even more painfully when he begins his account of the Sun and the Good, the Divided Line and the Cave. But here he insists at first that he is incapable of describing the Good and can only tell of its offspring, the Sun. This, too, is an unsatisfactory solution, since he clearly still knows something and that is enough to undermine his claims to ignorance.

No one reading the *Republic* for the first time notices any of this as they read of Socrates' brainwave about natural human aptitudes. Even a first-time reader particularly sensitive to the problems of Socratic irony will notice only that here Socrates advances an original and positive notion. That reader can have no sense at this stage in the dialogue of how much will flow from this positive notion. It is only after we read the whole dialogue, and then turn back to locate its crucial moments, that this moment of the brainwave gains its significance. We see several things. Like logic and computers, Socrates' dialectic produces nothing it has not been fed. The beauty of the dialectic as we have it on the page is that the task of separating out all the propositions of which it is composed has already been done for us. The seminal proposition about aptitudes is highlighted for us by Socrates' oath and his claiming that he had only thought of it at that moment.

The proposition about aptitudes is significant because much else hangs from it and all of it is tightly woven together. The exaggerated casualness with which this huge card is laid upon the table is a *litotes* or understatement, and Plato can only get away with it the first time. Thereafter readers know exactly what kind of trick is being pulled on them here and relish every instant of it. Especially the 'By Zeus.' It is as though the elaborate off-handedness which introduces this crucial notion is Plato's acknowledgement of the careful readers' pains, and a marker that this moment is indeed crucial.

🌴

These four jokes of Plato are a more or less arbitrary selection, though no one, I think, could go past Socrates' proposal for a pension. They are sophisticated jokes: all four turn on a complex logical play. So Socrates' denunciation of dramatic art comes from a character in a dramatic dialogue. This is a contradiction between what is said and how it is said, and springs from a logic which we recognize from Kant who called self-referring propositions which validated themselves transcendental propositions. Socrates' denunciation of dramaturgy is a transcendental contradiction. Again, Socrates' aping of Protagoras' pretensions about sophistry is a logical *reductio ad absurdum* in which Socrates parodies Protagoras' rhetorical trickery to make claims even more implausible. This is one of the few places in the dialogues in which Socrates makes claims he knows to be untrue. And the reason for this departure from his normal practice is clear to us.

The third joke in the courtroom is much more dramatic than the first two because Socrates is in mortal danger. Much of its power comes from this. Its logical form is the paradox. We think of those jurors waiting to hear from Socrates what penalty he proposed for himself and we imagine the shock they felt when they heard. We feel it ourselves. In part the humor is seeing those jurors take a pratfall. Of course, after that shock, Anytus and Meletus and Lycon must have been delighted at Socrates' insolence. The trial itself is comic as Plato handles it because it is a clash of humors. The jury cannot understand Socrates. But he understands both them and himself very well, so the clash is only partial. Socrates plays on it constantly. As for the logical play of the fourth joke, it turns on the practice of Socratic irony, that characteristic self-effacement which could on occasion drive a respondent to fury.

We may define the logical element in these four jokes more precisely. After all most jokes are a play on logic or words. All four of these jokes also share a characteristic absurdity. So the first has a character in a dramatic dialogue who is opposed to dramaturgy in principle; the second is a *reductio ad absurdum*; the third is the proposal of an absurd penalty; and the fourth is an absurd claim to spontaneity and improvisation. This element in Plato's writing, a love of absurdity, he shared with Aristophanes. But the jokes are also exercises in logical reasoning and contextual analysis. They remind us that Plato's student Aristotle produced one of the most elaborate and exact disquisitions on logical form in our era. Logical fallacy and its detection were major parts of rhetoric. Protagoras developed a distinct science of argumentation which was neither quite logical nor concerned with truth but only with the most superficial verbal victories. He called this eristic, and Plato himself wrote a dialogue more or less in this style, the *Euthydemus*.

The ancient Athenians who were contemporary with Plato, his earliest readers, were sophisticated in the techniques of logical argumentation, to a degree that we are not. I think that his first readers would have seen these jokes much more readily than we do. And this brings us at last to the real point of this essay. Humor, like music, is universal for the most part and once we see the humor in these passages of Plato, it is hard to unsee it. But if they are humorous, then the level of self-awareness and subtlety at which Plato is writing is higher than is commonly assumed. There is a tendency very natural to modern scholars to suppose that any differences between their understandings and Plato's understandings should be put down to a failure on Plato's part. If Plato believes X in some instance and we believe Y, the only question is: how did Plato come to make this mistake? This is not a helpful assumption when we consider the Dialogues. We are already running at some distance behind them.

Hypnosophy

A MONG THE MORE absurd philosophies of antiquity was that of the Hypnosophists, a sect of late though uncertain date and of obscure origins. One of their central doctrines, that the sun is new every day, is to be found in exactly this form among the extant fragments of Heraclitus of Ephesus (c. 500 BC). But the use made of this proposition by the Hypnosophists has only a tenuous relationship to Heracliteanism in any of its forms. There is some evidence that the Hypnosophists thought themselves heirs of Eleatic teaching.

According to the Hypnosophists the sun is literally new every day and entirely different in substance from the sun of the day before or of the day after. This claim met with the reasonable objection that to say that the sun is new every day is to contradict oneself since one mentions a single sun, 'the sun', which is at the same time asserted to be different each day; to claim, on the other hand, that there is a new sun every day would avoid this criticism at least. To this mild objection the Hypnosophist Creontiades replied that in country villages it was often claimed that the milk was fresh every day. But it would be nothing short of a miracle if this were literally true, and it was exactly the same milk, drop for drop, which magically reconstituted itself every day and refreshed itself. Of course it is milk different in substance each day which, it is claimed, appears fresh on the doorstep at dawn. And so with the sun. It is as absurd to suppose that it is substantially the same sun each day as that it is the same milk, and only a fool would be misled by the elliptical expression.

This preposterous defence of the Hypnosophist position could not, in any case, defend a corollary of their view of the sun. This was that every day one of the stars which shone in the night sky served as that day's sun from rising to setting, after which it returned to its place among the stars. The stars of the night sky are all suns of days to come or days past, seen simultaneously in a clear sky during darkness. They believed that there are some thirty six thousand visible stars, corresponding to the number of days in a lifetime of a hundred years.

The notion that the stars are the suns of a lifetime's days underlay their reason for calling themselves Hypnosophists or 'Sleep-sages.' They supposed that the stars in the night sky are exactly analogous to the state of the sleeping mind. Each day of that mind's life is simultaneously available as immediate experience to the mind in deep sleep. This proposition, they argued, was demonstrably true since under hypnosis susceptible subjects may be brought by regression to a full account of any moment in their past lives. As for future days, these too are accessible to eternal spirits, but they are difficult to remember since all premonitions are experienced from the point of view of those future dates on which they occur, and not from the point of view of the viewer presently. Premonitions are necessarily obscure because they diverge from our present point of view in ways we have not experienced in the waking life.

It follows that for Hypnosophists the knowledge enjoyed by the sleeping mind is much more extensive than that of the mind awake. The mind asleep can at will recreate any moment of its past or future in perfect detail. But if the mind in deep sleep and in potential possession of its entire experience does, indeed, take up one option and enter into a moment of its past or future, then it reverts from a state of total self-possession to an actual and necessarily limiting moment. In the same way the observer of a clear night sky may turn from a contemplation of the entire panoply to a consideration of just one star among them all, and thereby cease to see the whole. This the Hypnosophists supposed to be the transition from deep sleep to the dreaming state. The perception of the whole, which is deep sleep, is beyond any temporal succession since all moments are presently available for immediate experience equally. The being in deep sleep is inviolable and immortal and has neither past nor future, beginning nor end. It is at this point that the Hypnosophists claim an Eleatic succession, freely quoting from Parmenides' Way of Truth: neither was (being) nor will it be, since it is now, altogether, one and continuous.

Troeschler has explored affinities between Hypnosophy and the

Hindu Gymnosophists whom they resemble in name. In Hinduism wisdom is regarded as a fourth state which is simultaneously inclusive of the waking, dreaming and deep sleep states. Troeschler points to the significance of the seed syllable AUM in the Upanishads though not in the Vedas. In the later work these three letters of the syllable correspond to the waking, dreaming and deep sleep states, and the repetition of the syllable is believed to aid the realization of the fourth state. Despite Troeschler it is doubtful that the psychological doctrines of the Hypnosophists have any more claim on Eastern teaching than they do on Heraclitus or Parmenides. Evans has argued that the astronomical doctrines deliberately exploited paradox to engage the interest of seekers in the psychological theory. Against this must be set the maxim of Demos, Creontiades' successor, that just as there was no way to understand being awake and being asleep except through their analogies in the heavens, so equally were the heavenly lights incomprehensible except as symbols of the processes governing the animal and vegetable consciousness.

Hypnosophists developed theories about the relations between sleeping and healing. They supposed that the narrowing of focus from the breadth of the sleeping mind, which is required for the waking life, is strenuous and tires the subject, making a return to the undifferentiated principle a necessity. At the other tropic of the process, the accumulation of energy through reunion with the divine principle in sleep required its discharge in another day of waking life. The energy acquired through sleep is responsible during sleep for growth and healing, during the waking phase for physical activity and for mental attentiveness. Later schismatic Hypnosophists claimed that it was not one star in particular which served as the sun, a different one each day, but all the stars together which then burst asunder again to form the night stars. In this way, they claimed, each day and even each moment of the waking consciousness contains potentially the entire experience of the subject. This confers upon each waking moment its stamp of unavoidable necessity and solidity, and its infinitude of organized detail. There are two selves, the greater and the less, of which the greater contains the world within itself, and the other is contained within the world.

The similarities between Hypnosophist Psychology and Leibniz's monadology have been widely discussed. Schiaparelli has claimed to detect elements of Hypnosophist doctrine in John Keats' "Endymion" and "Ode to Psyche". The refusal of the Hypnosophists to accommodate the established discoveries of astronomy in their own age is similar to the Romantic distrust of Enlightenment science in theirs. In both cases these reactionaries failed to realize or revolted against their being alive during a period of unequivocal scientific progress. Their refusal to recognize this progress rendered their opposition to it obsolete almost before it was offered. We may compare to Hypnosophy William Blake's ludicrous belief that the sun was at the bottom of his garden at the end of a long stick. But the Romantics, in their return to an already outmoded conception of the world, expressed their sentiments in the poignant colors of poetry, painting and music. This cannot be said of the Hypnosophists so far as we may know them from their fragments, which are without literary merit. An exception may be this short poem, unattributed in the Anthology and given here in the lively half-rhymes of Rev. Grube:

> How glorious I when Justice once
> Rapt me past desk, room, city, space
> Into divinest darkness, bade me dance
> Across the stars
>
> Ten thousand crystal corridors alight,
> I turned and there ten thousand more,
> The doors of every memory flung wide
> And I was where?
>
> All moments, places, dreamt or known
> Were closer then than where I sat.
> When I looked with my eyes at the dim room
> I laughed at it.

A Chinese Way of Work

Thism essay retells and examines three very short stories about the crafts from ancient China. These stories concern a butcher, a wheelwright and a gardener, and their source is the *Chuang Tzu* of about 300 BC. The *Chuang Tzu* belongs to the school of philosophical Taoism, so called to distinguish it from many other forms of Taoism. The prime work of philosophical Taoism is *The Way and Its Power,* and I begin my account of the butcher with a quotation from it.

I.
The Butcher

In the forty third chapter of *The Way and Its Power* is this proposition:

> Only the nonexistent can penetrate the impenetrable.

It must be stressed that this is only one possible translation of the five Chinese characters here. *The Way and Its Power* has been translated into English more often than any other work. Still, this translation is an elegant paradox. It has the clear and simple logical form: only X can Y. Nonetheless, after one moment's thought, the proposition turns out to be mindstoppingly incomprehensible. Partly this is the effect of the double negative, the 'non' of nonexistent and the 'im' of impenetrable. The proposition is itself as impenetrable as what it describes. It appears immediately after the claim that what is most submissive conquers what is hardest, and perhaps takes that notion to its extreme logical conclusion: the ultimately submissive is the nonexistent and the ultimately hard is the impenetrable.

My wife who is Chinese tells me that the proposition describes the relation between the spiritual and the material realms: what is materially nonexistent is the spirit and what is impenetrable is matter. This, I think, must be right. But quite another reading is suggested by a more or less contemporary work to *The Way and Its Power*. Here is a cook called Ting talking to Lord Wen-hui about butchery in the *Chuang Tzu*:

> A good cook changes his knife once a year—because he cuts. A mediocre cook changes his knife once a month—because he hacks. I've had this knife of mine for nineteen years and I've cut up thousands of oxen with it, and yet the blade is as good as though it had just come from the grindstone. There are spaces between the joints, and the blade of the knife has really no thickness. If you insert what has no thickness into such spaces, then there's plenty of room—more than enough for the blade to play about in. That's why after nineteen years the blade of my knife is still as good as when it first came from the grindstone.
>
> However, whenever I come to a complicated place, I size up the difficulties, tell myself to watch out and be careful, keep my eyes on what I'm doing, work very slowly, and move the knife with the greatest subtlety, until—flop! The whole thing comes apart like a clod of earth crumbling to the ground.[1]

Ting supposes that the blade of the knife has no thickness on this translation. But this description would fit the edge of the knife better than the whole blade, and it is the edge and not the blade which is as good as if it had just come from the grindstone. The finer the edge the more it tends to non-existence; the more it becomes non-existent, the harder the material it can cut. And an ox is surely as solid as you are likely to find. But in fact there is no cutting. The sharpness of the edge is never compromised and so it always remains perfectly sharp. Instead, Ting waves his arm like a magician describing figures with his wand in the air, and the ox falls to pieces before our eyes. The blade's very edge touches nothing, but finds the secret apertures in the flesh. The sides of the blade very gently part those openings just a little more. But it is enough.

We cannot really call Ting a butcher because he no longer cuts anything. This reminds me of a story my father told me. When he

---

1. *The Complete Works of Chuang Tzu, The Secret of Caring for Life,* Trans: Burton Watson, 1970, Columbia University Press, chap. 3, p. 51.

was home on holidays from school, he used to work with the family firm of joiners. On one occasion they were building a double stair-case in the two-storey hall of a manor house in Berkshire. This staircase was a wonder to my father. For it used no screws or nails or glue. It was entirely free-standing. The people who made it had as little title to be called joiners as Ting had to be called butcher. All they did was to shape the pieces and lay them next to each other.

Ting does not see the ox nor those joiners the staircase as I would see them. For me they are indeed impenetrable, solid, unitary masses. But for Ting and the joiners they are as much the gaps they know in them as the substance. Such is science. It renders everything pervious, pellucid. These people know these things thoroughly, through and through, inside out. I know only the appearance but they know the reality. No one knows everything expertly though the range of some seems superhuman. But collectively, it seems to me, humanity knows most of what surrounds it from within in this way. Craftworkers know the inwardness of what they handle and their knowledge too is that nonexistent which permeates the inside of things. At one level this is the spirit of which my wife was speaking. A systematic knowledge of grammar and logic would do the same for anyone reading this.

Ting does much less than most butchers because he does not cut. His technique, we might say, is minimalist. But it would be a mis-take to think that he has adapted that technique to spare himself effort. We shall read later of a gardener who goes to the very greatest trouble in order, as he thinks, to keep being buoyed up by the Tao. The reason why Ting acts as he does is because he wants to do the very least he can do to the world at the same time as achieving his ends. And the gardener likewise. It is a Taoist principle that only by doing the least you can to the world are you likely to have much success. So in *The Way and Its Power* governing an empire is like cooking a small fish which is easily damaged. The ruler is just a shadowy presence to his subjects and when he has achieved his goals, the people all say that it happened naturally. That inward knowledge allows everything to run with the least possible interfer-ence. It is a knowledge mingled with love and respect and not at all self-serving.

After listening to Cook Ting, we must remember that we are actually in a slaughter-house. The ancient Chinese seem to have been sensitive to the life of an ox. An emperor once from his palace heard the lowing of an ox. On enquiry, he learnt that the ox was on its way to the imperial slaughterhouse. He instructed that since he had heard it, he would eat no part of the animal. Cook Ting is engaged in very ugly work, and there is surely in this story something of that nasty pleasure which writers take in rubbing their readers' noses in what is vile. And the *Chuang Tzu* piles on the pressure at just this point, forcing us to see Ting's actions in the most unlikely terms:

> Cook Ting was cutting up an ox for Lord Wen-hui. At every touch of his hand, every heave of his shoulder, every move of his feet, every thrust of his knee—zip! zoop! He slithered the knife along with a zing, all was in perfect rhythm, as though he were performing the dance of the Mulberry Grove or keeping time to the Ching-shou music.[2]

This picture must have irked a good Confucian. How dare anyone compare a butcher at work to the ritual performances which so moved the Master that he could not eat for a week afterwards! But in fact Cook Ting is a model of piety. He says of himself that all he cares about is the Way. And he says this to his lord, and in this passage he becomes a moral example to the ruler. These are very strange and deliberate twists in the normal order of things. The lowest usurps the place of the highest in two distinctly different ways.

A scholar and gentleman is introduced to real spiritual knowledge by a working man: this is the form of all three of the stories in this essay. Taoism is radical and antinomian in this way but it is very far from revolutionary. In their education of their rulers, these lower members of society still keep their place and the rulers' acceptance of their teaching is the mark of their worthiness as rulers. But this said, I find it very hard to think of any other ancient civilization which wrote into its origins this reversal of power roles so explicitly, though both Christianity and Buddhism come to mind. It is notice-

2. Ibid., p. 50.

able that Ting claims only to care for the Tao, and the gardener later says that he is under instruction from a spiritual master. In the *Chuang Tzu* the craftworkers are often the spiritual centers, and it is through their crafts that they have gained their insight. Socrates too believed that the crafts conferred real knowledge. But Socrates lived in a democracy in which the craftsmen aspired to run the government, and Socrates had no time for this delusion. Cook Ting and the other craftsmen in the *Chuang Tzu* entertain no such dreams. They keep strictly to their strengths though we are amazed at the openness and authority with which they speak to their betters. But how the insight conferred by the craft is to be realized anew in the craft of kingship, this is a matter which these workers respectfully leave alone. It says much for freedom of speech in ancient China that workers should have been represented so.

And Socrates too believed that the crafts were spiritual. They required of the craftworker the contemplation of an invisible idea. To make a bed, a carpenter must contemplate the idea of the bed in the mind of God. But this formulation suffers from its separation of the ideal from the material, which is a recurrent weakness of Platonism. In the story of Cook Ting, his understanding of the ox is realized by those bloody hands in the very core and viscera of the beast. The spiritual understanding takes us directly into the material fact. But Ting has, he says, butchered thousands of oxen and his knowledge of this ox on the day comes from this immense experience, an idea of the ox though not one seen in heaven. Ting's knowledge of that composite ox invisibly pierces this ox before us which he is slaughtering, and he knows all its ways and joints and openings from within. The solidity of the ox is penetrated through and through and vanishes, leaving only the wonderful subtleties of its parts.

II.
The Wheelwright

Duke Huan was in his hall reading a book. The wheelwright P'ien, who was in the yard below chiseling a wheel, laid down his mallet and chisel, stepped up into the hall, and said to Duke Huan, "This book Your Grace is reading—may I venture to ask whose words are in it?"

"The words of the sages," said the duke.

"Are the sages still alive?"

"Dead long ago," said the duke.

"In that case, what you are reading there is nothing but the chaff and dregs of the men of old!"

"Since when does a wheelwright have permission to comment on the books I read?" said Duke Huan. "If you have some explanation, well and good. If not, it's your life!"

Wheelwright P'ien said, "I look at it from the point of view of my own work. When I chisel a wheel, if the blows of the mallet are too gentle, the chisel slides and won't take hold. But if they're too hard, it bites in and won't budge. Not too gentle, not too hard—you can get it in your hand and feel it in your mind. You can't put it into words, and yet there's a knack to it somehow. I can't teach it to my son, and he can't learn it from me. So I've gone along for seventy years and at my age I'm still chiseling wheels. When the men of old died, they took with them the things that couldn't be handed down. So what you are reading there must be nothing but the chaff and dregs of the men of old."[3]

In just a page the author here achieves a considerable tension. Will old P'ien's speech save him from execution? We are not told and so we weigh the explanation he gives of his behavior very carefully. In the case of Cook Ting and Lord Wen-hui, we must suppose that the Lord has deigned to visit his cook in the slaughterhouse, a signal favor. But old P'ien has disturbed the Duke at his reading and then insulted his devotion to the greatest literature of their nation. In the story of Cook Ting there was tension of another kind, between the savagery of Ting's work and the ritual dances. But here the tension is immediately between the two interlocutors.

I am hopeful that the Duke will spare old P'ien. He is seventy years old and the readiness with which the Duke answers P'ien's questions suggests a degree of closeness between them. But what could have induced the old man to take such a risk? From *The Way*

3. Op. cit., chap. 13, pp. 152–153.

and Its Truth onwards Taoists are more cautious than most philosophers in looking after themselves. P'ien, I suspect, has calculated this transaction with his master very carefully. He has worked out just how to say what has to be said and escape with his life. Not too soft, not too hard with his words as well as with chisel and mallet, Of course, he could not know how the Duke would reply to his questions, but almost any reading matter would have served for his condemnation.

Still, it seems spontaneous enough. There he is at work on the wheel, shaping away. Then he downs tools and steps into the hall. But he certainly has not forgotten what he was just doing because he refers to it very soon. My guess is that P'ien had pondered these matters a long time, but there was something about his working there that day with the Duke reading inside which flipped a switch and drove him to his temerity. And I can guess what it is. The demands of mallet and chisel, not too soft and not too hard, struck him irresistibly as a perfect parallel with the Duke's responsibilities as ruler and judge. Chinese political theory is much concerned with the appropriateness of rewards and punishments, from the harshness of the legalists to the laissez-faire of Mohists and Taoists. When P'ien says to the Duke that his books won't help him, he is saying that the Duke's duties demand a flair, a knack, exactly as his do. He could never have gained that touch from a book. He cannot even teach it to his son. And no more can the Duke. What the Duke requires to rule well and to judge justly is a sense as subtle and incommunicable as that.

Against the entire weight of Chinese scripture and scholarship, the five Classics, the four Books, we are to set a feeling in a wheelwright's fingers. His presumption is startling and we would acquiesce without a murmur in his being put down, if only with words. His position is the quintessence of working class anti-intellectualism. It is astonishing that this story should be part of the Chinese intellectual tradition. Heraclitus, Xenophanes and Plato had abused Homer, the first and greatest poet of their age, but they did not question the power of tradition. It was merely that Homer was not good enough. But with P'ien the whole process was in question. None of it mattered nor ever could.

But again P'ien is close to the thought of *The Way and Its Power* just as Cook Ting illustrated the penetrability of matter with his edge of no thickness. For there too the whole of learning is dismissed as worthless:

> Exterminate learning and there will no longer be worries.
> Between yea and nay
> How much difference is there?
> Between good and evil
> How great is the distance?[4]

In the heart of the Chinese tradition from very early times has been this questioning of the value of tradition itself and of the morality which depended upon it. The nearest parallel to this I can think of also comes from the East: if you meet the Buddha on the road, kill him. Of course, very recently in the West the Arts professoriate has done much to destroy the disciplines which it professes by trying the greatest of our works before the tribunal of absolute equality between classes, races, and genders. But even that anti-professoriate does not deny the power of education. Like those Greeks with Homer, they just dislike the content. But the Taoists are saying that the very idea of learning is a mistake, a needless confusion, a fiddling with the natural order of things. 'Book-burning' as liberation and in one of their most ancient texts! This touches upon one of the tenderest places in Chinese history as in our own.

Philosophical Taoism is a counterweight to the entirety of the Chinese literary tradition. It sets itself against the very idea of such a thing. And, of course, it is part of that tradition at the same time. For the Chinese, this massive and obvious incoherence seems to be perfectly acceptable. There is nothing incoherent in what P'ien says. He may be foolhardy and incorrigibly radical but he makes sense. But what about the person who wrote the story? If every such inscription gives us only the chaff and dregs, why bother? If the author approves P'ien's words, then his writing them down is inconsistent.

Inconsistent or not, this way of thinking has set the Chinese tradition apart from most others, and most especially from the tradi-

---

4. Lao Tzu, *Tao Te Ching XX*, tr.: D C. Lau, 1963, England, Penguin Books, p. 76.

tions of Roman law and Judaic law. Both of these attempt a comprehensive, if not exhaustive, series of prescriptions according to a systematic code of law. The Chinese did not do this. They found a way of maintaining an effective judiciary without the need for such an elaboration in writing. Though their education and training were literary to an exceptional degree, they eschewed this particular form of literature and administration. Yet their system of civil administration was one of the most long lasting of all. The tendency towards codification was there from the time of the Legalists onwards but it was tempered by Taoists. After one period under Legalism, the imperial court turned to philosophical Taoism to restore the balance. Taoism's distrust of the written word has played a part in the formation of a distinctively Chinese system of government.

P'ien, we might say, was born to be a wheelwright. That is why he feels it in his fingers and is still doing it at the age of seventy. P'ien trusts that just as there were people born to be wheelwrights before him, so there will be others born after him. So with the Duke and his task. If in time to come, nobody should be born with a flair for government and justice, then all the libraries in the world will not supply the lack. If, on the other hand, people with a flair for government continue to appear, then the writings of the ancients are redundant. This is recognizable as the world of the *Bhagavad Gita* or Plato's *Republic*. All the different kinds of people needed for a self-sufficient society appear generation by generation in accordance with the nature of things. The task is to ensure that those innate capacities and callings are honoured and used. It is emphatically not a matter of parental origins but of natural capacity. So it is in the *Gita* and in the *Republic* and here again, as P'ien tells the Duke that he cannot teach his son. P'ien trusts that in the nature of things there will be born wheelwrights and Dukes like themselves in the future as there have been in the past, that he lives in a providential order. It is as though for P'ien civilization is not a thin veneer which protects us from our brutal propensities. Civilization is what happens when you let go and let it all happen as it will. It is what is really there at the base of it all. The state withers away but not after the mechanization of production. It withers away because the rulers become so adept in their manipulation of circumstance that no one even notices that they are there. But this takes flair.

Compared to the call to exterminate learning, P'ien is tactful when he describes the scriptures of the sages as chaff and dregs. From the point of view of philosophical Taoism, traditions are serial abusers, since they attempt to impose upon later generations the will of earlier ones. They refuse to let go. C.S. Lewis has argued that industrialization is an unprecedented imposition by a few generations on the future, since it precludes the possibility of a pre-industrial life from all the generations to come. He calls this process the abolition of man, the limiting of human freedom to live as we choose, radically and finally. But the same is true of Roman and Judaic law, the codifications of earlier generations imposed upon those to come. And all quite unnecessary since the Way in its providence will supply everything needful. In the West the imposition of these legal codes spurred endless antinomian responses, but in the *Chuang Tzu* all of this was taken up in principle into the heart of the scholarly culture very early. From this point of view, we must say that Chinese civilization evinced a much greater faith in divine providence than those Western cultures which resorted to codes of law.

III.
The Gardener

Tzu-kung travelled south to Ch'u, and on his way back through Chin, as he passed along the south bank of the Han, he saw an old man preparing his fields for planting. He had hollowed out an opening by which he entered the well and from which he emerged, lugging a pitcher, which he carried out to water the fields. Grunting and puffing, he used up a great deal of energy and produced very little result.

"There is a machine for this sort of thing," said Tzu-kung. "In one day it can water a hundred fields, demanding very little effort and producing excellent results. Wouldn't you like one?"

The gardener raised his head and looked at Tzu-kung. "How does it work?"

"It's a contraption made by shaping a piece of wood. The back end is heavy and the front end light and it raises the water as though it were pouring it out, so fast that it seems to boil right over! It's called a well sweep."

The gardener flushed with anger and then said with a laugh, "I've heard my teacher say, where there are machines, there are bound to be machine worries; where there are machine worries, there are bound to be machine hearts. With a machine heart in your breast, you've spoiled what was pure and simple; and without the pure and simple, the life of the spirit knows no rest. Where the life of the spirit knows no rest, the Way will cease to buoy you up. It's not that I don't know about your machine—I would be ashamed to use it!"

Tzu-kung blushed with chagrin, looked down, and made no reply.[5]

East or West, this is the earliest story I know to criticize technological innovation in principle. And I presume that such criticism would have appeared as wrong-headed and tendentious to a Chinese reader in antiquity as to us. And so this story is comparable in its contrariety and heterodoxy to Ting's spiritual path of butchery and P'ien's downright rejection of literature. The author is careful to tell us that the old gardener's enormous efforts produce very little result, and the gardener is even ruder to the mandarin who accosts him than P'ien was to his Duke. And that mandarin had gone out of his way to do the poor old fellow a good turn.

The gardener and his teacher believe in the simple life to an unusual degree. Apart from the well, the pitcher is the old gardener's entire equipment in this phase of his operations. This, too, is the teaching of *The Way and Its Power* where the culture promoted is very primitive. So primitive, indeed, that even Cook Ting would be in trouble, since *The Way and Its Power* supposes that the incidence of sharpened tools and weapons is an index of the state's benightedness. Wheelwright P'ien would be all right, provided only that the wheels he made followed old ruts. Perhaps the old gardener here would be happiest in that first community which Socrates

5. *The Complete Works of Chuang Tzu, Heaven and Earth*, op. cit., chap. 12, p. 134.

imagines at the beginning of his quest for a just society.[6] In that earliest society the essentials are provided by the arts of agriculture, building, weaving and so on. They live in the simplest houses and eat the simplest food and spend most of their time drinking wine and singing hymns to the Gods. Socrates' companions object to this social order as fit only for pigs, but the gardener would approve.

Fifty years ago I found myself one evening in a Greek village square in summer. Some scores of villagers had gathered with their chairs, and the discussion concerned the village's adoption of a petrol-driven generator to provide electric lights. At that time they still used oil lamps, and many believed they should keep them. I had never before in England heard such an issue debated. In England the technology was just rolled out willy-nilly and it was never an issue. The imperative of progress was beyond discussion.

Unlike Cook Ting and wheelwright P'ien, the gardener is not named. Just as the work he is doing is much more rudimentary than theirs, so is he. And this is emphasized by the factitious detail which embellishes the telling, the name of the gardener's adviser, the name of his teacher, Confucius, and the place where the episode occurred. Of the gardener's teacher we learn nothing except the teaching but like the gardener he remains nameless. In these ways the gardener approaches more closely the condition of the uncarved block, formlessness, than do the cook and the wheelwright. Namelessness, indeed, is the property of the beginning of heaven and earth according to the very first chapter of *The Way and Its Power*. Later in this passage from the *Chuang Tzu* Confucius compares the gardener to Mr. Chaos, a primeval God to whom two well-wishers did a good turn. Every day they bored a hole in Mr. Chaos so that he could see, hear, eat, breathe and so on. But on the seventh day Mr. Chaos died. In the same way the gardener is primordial, a figure from a much earlier era in human development. But he has learnt how to cope effectively with Confucian philanthropists.

The gardener is angry when Tzu-kung describes the well-sweep but he controls himself and replies with the words of his teacher. His objection to the well-sweep is a series of propositions in which

6. Plato, *The Republic*, 370–373.

the last term of each provides the first term of the next. This method of argument is very common in *The Way and Its Power* and, there as here, it has a certain cumulative force. The critical notion here is the machine heart which is the result of having machine worries and which does away with what is pure and simple at the core of a person. When this is lost, so also is any confidence in the order of things, in providence. In the gardener's view, using machines has a harmful effect on the spirit and on faith. The Way normally buoys us up but when the spirit has been compromised, it will cease to do so.

What is the relation between the mechanization of work and spiritual faith? According to the gardener, machines bring machine worries, but are these worries more destructive of spiritual faith than the worries which accompany other possessions? There have been many rich societies in history but they were not, for the most part, atheistical. On the other hand industrialized societies do seem to tend this way. Certainly England was the first country to industrialize and its national church has severely contracted. There is a very general view in that country that belief in the divine is a stop gap for scientific and mechanical understandings and will eventually disappear.

Adoption of the well-sweep may bring the gardener worries. But the invention of the well-sweep must itself have required a machine-heart to bring the machine into existence. The mechanization of the European heart began before the Industrial Revolution and not because of it. Between 1600 and 1750, from Francis Bacon to David Hume, mechanical causes quite displaced spiritual ones. The new tools and new processes of industrialization were themselves the products of that shift in inquiry. This shift was a transference of attention from the physical world as divinely created to a much more detailed analysis of its actual operations.

What are the worries which make the machine-heart? We have met this concern with worries with the line 'Exterminate learning and there will no longer be worries.' There the avoidance of worry justified the destruction of learning; here it justifies banning all technological development down to and including the well-sweep. Using a well-sweep means having to think about it, its soundness, its fulcrum, its construction, the water-channels and so on. But the gardener's present activity requires no thinking much at all. It is arduous and long lasting, patient and mindless.

Let us place the people we have met so far in the *Chuang Tzu* in a line from left to right. On the extreme left let us place awareness of Tao as the *Chuang Tzu* imagines it. On the extreme right we place complete unawareness of Tao. Nearest to awareness of Tao on the left let us place the gardener's teacher; next to him, on his right, the gardener himself; on the right of the gardener, wheelwright P'ien and Cook Ting; on the right of these two, Lord Wen-hui; to his right, Duke Huan and Tzu-kung; to their right, Confucius himself.

The goal is mindlessness, a complete absence of all concerns so that our natures return to being pure and simple, blissfully trusting in the powers which bear us up in our being. But this mindlessness has its own disciplines and activities and leads closer and closer to Tao, through a number of distinct phases. In the *Chuang Tzu* each of these phases has a more extravagant name than the last and they must mark the intervals on the line before the awareness of Tao at its extremity. Even the gardener has achieved considerable proficiency in this practice if not in well-sweeps. He later tells Tzu-kung:

> You would do best to forget your spirit and breath, break up your body and limbs—then you might be able to get somewhere.[7]

This sounds distinctly shamanic.

✽

It is hard to talk of the spirit. We need a vocabulary which is already known to our hearers. God, spirit, soul, eternity, providence, heaven, hell, all presuppose an earlier acquaintance on the part of our audience. This is very constricting, a tight suit which the spirit would rather not wear. Theology is much worse than scripture in this respect, one of those codifications of which we have supposed the Chinese to be largely free. Like the Christian New Testament, the *Chuang Tzu* denies that the letter is an adequate vehicle for the

---

7. *The Complete Works of Chuang Tzu,* op. cit., p. 135.

spirit. Learning is not enough and it is often itself the barrier to understanding. Look at Tzu-kung and Confucius. More than most scriptures, those of the Taoists resist the inertia of an accomplished literary theocracy.

A spiritual working class is one foundation of a stable society. Socrates and Plato thought work to be both contemplative and active, and this gift of contemplation extended to all the crafts and professions. In the Gospel, parables of the crafts illuminate inwardness. In the *Chuang Tzu* peasants and artisans become teachers to scholars and lords. Ting, P'ien and the gardener are vivid spiritual beings, like the aged carpenter in Plato's *Republic* who will continue to work though sick because not to work is not to live. From any other point of view, the old gardener here is a very poor thing, but he is the one with access to realms of which we barely know the names.

www.ingramcontent.com/pod-product-compliance
Lightning Source LLC
Chambersburg PA
CBHW022008080426
42733CB00007B/529